Revised

Families

Applications of Social Learning to Family Life

Gerald R. Patterson
Department of Special Education,
University of Oregon
and Oregon Research Institute

Research Press
2612 North Mattis Avenue
Champaign IL 61820

ISBN 0-87822-156-5

Cover photography/Frank Moore

To Dr. Christianson, who made it possible to "see." To my mother and other friends who taught me what to look at.

Foreword

This book does not propose to explain everything that people do. Reading and putting into practice the procedures outlined here will not solve all of the problems that arise in your family. However, the concepts and procedures outlined here do constitute a means by which each of us, parent and child alike, can design and change many aspects of the world in which we live.

A person's behavior is shaped by his past as well as by his immediate experiences. Understanding how this happens puts the individual in a position to partially control his own behavior—a position of dignity. *Families* concerns itself with the details, the technology as it were, of how a person goes about changing his own behavior and the behavior of the people around him.

Living with Children and now *Families* depict a gradual evolution of this social learning technology. The first book might be thought of as a primer, in that it presents only the bare outlines of these developments. *Families,* on the other hand, more extensively describes more recent developments in behavior change technology.

Since publication of the first volume, the author has been privileged to work with such colleagues as Roberta Ray, David Shaw, Joe Cobb, Hy Hops, Steve Johnson, Robert Weiss, John Reid, Karl Skindrud, Richard Jones, Robert Conger, Matt Fleischman, and Al Levine. As a group we have had extensive experience in observing many normal and problem families, and each of us has been totally involved in applying the principles of social learning in assisting families who are having difficulties. The problems we have encountered range from child management problems to marital conflicts.

These investigations have been extensively reported in scientific journals (e.g., Patterson, McNeal, Hawkins, and Phelps, 1967) and in books (e.g., Patterson and Cobb, 1971a; Patterson, Cobb, and Ray, 1971). However, *Families*, written for the parent and the practitioner, contains the details of the procedures which cannot be presented in scientific papers. A film (Oregon Research Institute, 1974) has also been prepared to give a brief overview of the social learning approach to family intervention, and for the practitioner there is a detailed clinical manual (Patterson, Conger, Reid, and Jones, 1975) which should be mastered before implementing these procedures in a professional setting. Though some individuals could read this book and effectively institute the procedures toward altering the social environment, it has been our experience that the changes proceed more smoothly when carried out under the supervision of a trained behavior modifier. (This collaboration seems necessary if any family member is displaying high rates of deviant behavior.)

As we learn more about the social learning approach to behavior change, appropriate revisions and additions will be made in *Families*. Since its first publication in 1971, we've had extensive experience in working with children who steal. It has also been possible to develop and field-test materials appropriate for parents of normal preschool children. The changes made in the 1975 revision reflect these experiences. We are currently working with both normal families and those of adolescent delinquents. Future revisions of *Families* will undoubtedly reflect the outcome of these new experiences. In this sense, *Families* is perhaps not a book. Rather, it is a changing summary resulting from the interchanges between real families on one hand and social learning theorists on the other. Each has much to learn and much to give.

Contents

Introduction:
People as Agents of Behavior Change

This book is about the whole family—the people in it, what they do to each other, and how they do it. And most importantly, it outlines procedures which families can use to change themselves.

This book is written for parents and for other people who need to know how families "work." It describes the practical application of social learning principles to problems with which we are all familiar. The general principles have been developed by such writers as Skinner (1953), Bandura and Walters (1963), and Ullmann and Krasner (1969). *Living With Children* is a primer in social learning principles, emphasizing their application to some child management problems. *Families* is a more detailed outline of child management procedures and it also extends the applications to other family members including adolescents and parents.

The general process by which people change is the prime focus of this book. Children change over time; adults do too. *Children change their parents, just as the parents contribute to the changes in their children.* How does this happen? Section I outlines a social learning explanation of how parents and children go about the *normal* process of changing each other. Practical procedures necessary for changing behavior are detailed in Section II. In Section III, the pro-

1

cedures are applied in changing the behavior of both the older and the very young members of the normal family. Section IV describes the details of how to work with the preadolescent child who steals or is very aggressive.

People can use the principles of social learning theory to cope with everyday problems of family behavior management. How do you teach an eighteen-month-old child to eat something besides dessert? How do you teach a six-year-old child to go to bed when you ask him to? How do you teach a mother to stop nagging and scolding all the time? How do you train a father to come out from behind his newspaper? How do you negotiate with an adolescent about the use of the family car? How do you teach yourself and your spouse to stop fighting with each other? All of these problems require that we understand how to change the behavior of another person, and how to change our own behavior. In this approach it is the parents and other family members, not the professional, who are the key agents of behavior change in the family. Throughout this book, the emphasis is upon all of the family members being involved in changing the family environment. It is they who decide what behaviors to change. It is they who design the means of bringing it about.

Reading this Book

This book follows the programmed instruction format, in which the main ideas are carefully broken down into small steps and arranged in logical sequence. The format requires that you actively participate in the learning process by *responding* to the material, not by just passively reading the words. From this point on you will encounter an occasional sentence in which you will find a blank and a number 1_____. Write the number and what you think is an appropriate answer on lined scratch paper. Actually writing the responses helps you remember the material. After you have written your answer, check it with the answers provided at the bottom of the page. When you make an error, don't bother to erase your answer but simply write the correct answer beneath it. Be sure to record your own response before you check it against the correct answer.

A name and date refer to references listed at the end of the volume. This additional material explores a given point in greater detail than would be possible in a book like this one. Your local library or bookstore could help you in obtaining the additional material.

Key ideas found in each section will be listed again at the end of that section. For instance, the key ideas found in this section are listed below. The most important key idea in the Introduction is that parents change the behavior of children and children 1_____ the behavior of parents. Section I describes just how it is that most behavior change occurs in the normal family.

Key Ideas in the Introduction

Parents and children change each other's behavior.
Behavior change can be designed.

1. change

Section I
SOCIAL LEARNING: KEYS TO BEHAVIOR CHANGE

Mrs. S smiled at her two-year-old Cam and said, "What is this?" as she touched her hair. Cam grinned and said, "Hair," and then stood very still as he watched to see what his mother would do next. She seemed very pleased with his answer and said, "Oh my, Cam, you *are* a good rememberer. But what is this?" and she touched her nose. Cam was becoming very excited as he shouted, "Nose!" and ran to his mother, who picked him up and hugged him.

In teaching her son to use words, Mrs. S is using a process familiar to all parents—she is using a great many rewards. But Cam is training his mother just as surely as she is training him—he is rewarding her for being a good teacher. Actually, they are changing each other. This process of people changing each other goes on all of the time.

Much of our behavior represents the outcome of what we have learned from other people. *People teach people.* They teach each other how to talk. They teach each other when to smile, what clothes to wear, when to have a temper tantrum, how to read, when to fight, how to work, and when to kiss someone they love. These are social skills that are learned by observing and reacting to other people. "Social learning" is a term that describes this process.

In the social 1_____ process both persons are changed. The changes are small but they tend to accumulate over time. The children in the classroom are altered by the teacher, but they in turn change his behavior. Parents teach their children many social skills; in the process they themselves are changed by their children. We learn social behaviors from other 2_____ . *When two people interact, they both change.*

Another point is necessary to consider before discussing just how this process works. It may be easy to see how we can teach other people pro-social behaviors such as hugging, working, touching, or reading. However, it is also true that perfectly reasonable parents can *accidentally* teach their children all kinds of problem behaviors and not even notice that they have done so. Parents can teach their children to have temper tantrums or to whine and cry each night at bedtime. By their behavior other parents allow their children to learn to set fires, to steal, to suck their thumbs, to take the family car whenever they like, or to live only on peanut butter sandwiches. Most parents, of course, *say* they do not want their children to do these things. But observing what they *do* when they interact with their children often shows parents that this is in fact what they are teaching. One of the functions of this book is to train parents so that they understand just what it is they are teaching their children to do.

A child, on the other hand, can train his parents to nag, scold, and even spank him! These are certainly not the parent behaviors he would choose. Nevertheless, these are the problem behaviors he trains his parents to display. *Both pro-social and 3_____ behaviors are taught by people close to you* (Skinner, 1953). Unless you learn to take the time to observe what is going on, then you simply will not understand much about yourself or the people with whom you live. Parents change each other and their children, and children change their parents, but most people do not know that

1. learning   2. people   3. problem

they are being changed or that they are themselves agents of change. The blind are leading the blind.

Key Ideas in the Introduction to Section I

Social learning theory is concerned with how people teach people.
When two people interact, they both change.
Both pro-social and problem behaviors are learned.

1

Social Reinforcers

Why people act the way they do is something all of us talk about—like the weather; but like the weather it is something most of us really know very little about. The key concept of this book is that there is a useful explanation for much of our behavior, an explanation that seems, at first, just "too simple."

The Principle of Reinforcement

Much seemingly complex human behavior can be understood in terms of a person's efforts to maximize rewards and to minimize pain (Skinner, 1953). When applied to your own life, such an idea seems to be an overly simplified account of what really goes on. For example, your salary, food, or various prizes could be thought of as rewards, and illness and physical pain might be punishment. But it is just not reasonable to suppose that these things have much to do with a person's "personality." Money is a reward and physical pain is a punishment, but they probably have little to do with the learning of most social behaviors. The rewards and punishments that govern most social behaviors are much more subtle, and, since they are so close at hand, are almost invariably overlooked by persons attempting to understand their own behavior and that of their child.

Let's begin with the general idea and then go on to its practical implications. There are many things that can function as a reward, or "reinforcer," and they all have one thing in common. *When a behavior is followed by a reinforcer, the behavior is strengthened.* This means that the behavior is more likely to occur again in the future.

If you reinforce a child as soon as he finishes mowing the lawn, then he is more likely to mow the lawn again. If you forget to reinforce him, he is less likely to do it again. Reinforcers 1_____ behavior.

Mrs. S placed Cam down on the floor, saying, "All right, now, ready, set, go!" Cam raced over, touched the wall, and shot back to his mother with all the speed his stubby legs could muster. She clapped her hands and, with a surprised expression on her face, exclaimed, "Wow! You are back already!" No basketball star ever acknowledged the crowd's acclaim with greater nonchalance than did Cam. She gave him a hug and then stepped back expectantly as she got ready to repeat the game.

There is a great deal of reinforcement occurring here, but little of it has anything to do with the things that come to mind when we speak of rewards. No money changed hands; no prizes were given. The reinforcers that occurred here were *social* in nature. They are found only in the behavior of another person. Unlike money there is an endless supply; even if you give a lot of social reinforcers, you will not run out.

The first clear-cut social reinforcer in the example above was the hand-clapping when Cam returned from his run. Then there was the pleased expression on his mother's face,

1. strengthen

and her saying "Wow! You are back already!" These 2_____ strengthened his behaviors associated with the game. In the future when Mrs. S asks Cam to play the "ready, set, go" game, he will be more likely to do it.

During the game Cam frequently ran over and hugged his mother around her legs; sometimes he would smile and laugh. These things are also social 3_____ which strengthen the mother's behavior. Let's suppose that Cam simply marched dully through the game, not even glancing at his mother. No hugs, no smiles, no laughing countenance—by failing to reinforce his mother, he would decrease the likelihood that they would play such games again. If this happened very often he would train his mother not to play with him at all.

Social Reinforcers

The most powerful reinforcers for a child or an adult are found in the behaviors of another person. *The "little things," the close attention of another person, a touch, words of approval, a smile, a glance, or a kiss, are all examples of* 4_____ *reinforcers.*

These reinforcers cost nothing to give. They occur hundreds of times each day. You are being reinforced in almost every interaction that occurs during your day. You in turn are reinforcing your friends and acquaintances. If you are talking and your friend listens to you, the social reinforcer which you receive is your friend's 5_____ . When he stops listening and begins to look around the room you will probably stop talking and let him take his turn while you listen. If you watch closely, you will notice that there are definite traffic signals indicating when each of you is to begin and when you are to stop. Almost always there is a fair trade in that each of you reinforces the other at an almost equal rate (Patterson and Reid, 1970).

2. reinforcers   3. reinforcers   4. social   5. listening

There are some persons who just seem naturally good at reinforcing other people. They have the knack of making others glad to be around them. This is a skill that can be learned. First, remember to reinforce the other person by using praise and approval occasionally. Don't be a miser—reinforce once in a while. In addition, pay close attention to what he is saying. Look at the other person as he talks. Some people have "roving eyes"—they simply are not a good audience. Give the other person your full attention. Touch people once in a while. Touching, smiling, and kissing are beautiful reinforcers. All of these things can be learned.

Each friend teaches you what it is that you should talk to him about. He does this by being interested in only some of the things that you generally talk about, and not others. For some of the topics you ordinarily talk about he listens closely; for others he tends to become bored rather quickly. You train your friends and they train you. Notice that each of your friends has trained you to talk about slightly different topics. As a test of these notions, try to introduce a new topic into the conversation and note how quickly the conversation drifts back to the same old subject. Being trained to talk to a friend about things that interest him is a small thing. Nevertheless, in a very real sense, both you and your friend have changed each other.

Social Reinforcers at Work

A single reinforcement does not produce dramatic, long-term changes in behavior. Rather, it takes hundreds of reinforcements, consistently given, before long-term changes can be observed. For example, suppose a wife wanted to teach her husband to take some interest in the household budget. She would have to raise the subject each night and listen attentively while her husband responded. She would have to ignore most other topics introduced by her husband. I have observed a number of wives trained by such a process who find themselves in the odd position of talking night after night about their husband's work because it was the only topic that would bring him out from behind his newspaper. If the wife wanted to receive any reinforcement at all, she had to introduce these same topics night after night.

Behavior changes; but *changes in behavior are gradual and are most likely to occur if reinforcement is consistent.* If you try to teach your child to hang up his coat when he comes home in the evening, there are several things to consider. First, of course, it helps to have good models for behavior (Bandura and Walters, 1963). If both parents hang up their clothes, that increases the likelihood that the child might try to do the same. However, even if both parents were perfect models, it would not insure their child's being similar. Having excellent models makes it more likely that the child will "try it too." But when he tries it, he must be 6 _____ if the behavior is to occur consistently.

Even if both parents use the "windmill technique," throwing their clothes into random corners, they could still teach their child to hang up his clothes. It would be necessary only to provide a prompting cue such as "Please hang up your clothes." When he complies, supply an immediate social reinforcer such as "Thank you." This is a behavior you wish to strengthen. Remember to notice it when it occurs and to reinforce it. Just one reinforcement will not bring about a long-term change. It is more likely to take several weeks of consistent reinforcement on your part. Once he has learned to hang up his clothes and does it all of the time, then you can begin to cut down the reinforcement schedule. But long-term changes occur slowly and primarily as a result of 7 _____ social reinforcements.

Track yourself as a reinforcing agent. For the next twenty-four hours note the number of times that you use such social reinforcers as approving, touching, hugging, or listening attentively. Put down a mark by the name of the family member to whom you give a reinforcer each time you do so. At the end of the day you will have a rough notion of just how reinforcing you are and to whom you direct the

6. reinforced · 7. many, consistent

reinforcers. Many parents are surprised to find that they do not tend to reinforce people, or that one person "gets it all." It is not difficult to change this, but as a first step observe yourself and collect the data. *Observation and data collection are the first steps in changing behavior.*

Suppose that you find that you just do not reinforce other people very much. One thing that you might do is set up a daily practice session that would last for just thirty minutes. During that time, go on with your work, but every five minutes stop what you are doing and find one thing for which you can reinforce another person. Then return to what you were doing until another five minutes have gone by.

After four or five practice sessions, you should notice that other family members begin to reinforce you at a higher rate. If you give more reinforcement to others, you will receive more from them (Homans, 1961). "You get what you give"—this is one saying that research evidence supports. Keep in mind that these changes will come about gradually. You may have to do a good deal of giving before you notice that other family members are giving, too.

Some parents have found the dinner table to be an excellent practice situation. During the thirty minutes that the family is together, it is generally possible to give at least one reinforcer to each family member.

People differ in their reinforcing styles. Some people are miserly in their use of social reinforcers; others have a kind of "sandwich approach" in which a criticism is slipped in between several reinforcers.

The children come to the kitchen one by one and sit down at the table. Mr. C looks very closely at each of them but says nothing and begins passing the food around. The family's approach to supper is reminiscent of a group of loggers rushing through the first helping in order to get seconds, with no social amenities along the way.

Mr. C breaks the silence by saying, "You came when you were called tonight, Craig. That was good." After a pause he adds, "You forgot to wash your face and hands." At this point he launches into a long lecture about Craig's being generally sloppy and ill-mannered. . . .

While the father was trying to use social reinforcers, his style would not strengthen Craig's coming to the table when he is called. A reinforcer must not be a sugar-coating for punishment. If you suspect you are one of the many parents who use this technique, you might have your spouse or even one of the children count this behavior for you. The best way to gain control over your own behavior is to 8_____ it yourself or have someone else observe it for you. Do not just observe it, but record it as well. 9_____ and 10_____ _____ are the first steps in changing behavior.

In planning our environment we will want to strengthen new behaviors so that they will occur more often. But part of the problem may also involve weakening already existing behaviors so they will occur less often. *To weaken problem behaviors, you can use nonreinforcement or punishment, or reinforce something that will take the place of the problem behavior.*

Suppose that you and your six-year-old have trained each other so that he has become completely helpless when he is getting ready for school in the morning. The same child who can take his bicycle apart and put it back together again is for some reason unable to find his shirt in the morning. Even if you put it on for him, he seems unable to button it. While later in the day he has the agility and stamina of an Olympic decathlon champion, he is listless, aimless, and complains of sore throats and sundry aches and pains when he has to get ready for school. He has trained his mother to hover in constant attendance, find his shirt, tie his shoelaces, comb his hair, and even feed him in order to get him to school on time. By being so helpless, he forces his mother to do everything for him. When she finds his clothes, dresses him, and feeds

8. count, observe   9. Observation   10. data collection

him, she is *accidentally* 11_____ him for being helpless. On the other hand, she feels that if she doesn't do these
things he will be late for school. People will label her as a bad
mother. Just how does the social learning process work on a
real problem like this?

First, observe for several mornings. What specific things
have you been trained to do for him? Then weaken the helpless behaviors, and at the same time strengthen behaviors
which are related to his taking care of himself. When he does
something for himself you must be certain to reinforce him:
"Hey, you found your shirt; that's a big boy." To weaken the
helplessness requires simply that you do not reinforce it. He
may even be late to school for a few days. When this
happens, arrange a consequence for being late. The "punishment" should be a natural consequence such as "No TV at
night when you have been late for school." The list of natural
reinforcers which you can withdraw is very long: for
example, desserts at night, the right to ride the bicycle, or the
right to leave the yard after school.

When he is helpless, don't reinforce him. If this results
in his being late, the punishment could be the removal of a
reinforcer that he has been taking for granted.

When you begin such a program, you must remember to
be consistent. If the child is occasionally in such a hurry that
you feel you must help him dress and thus reinforce his
helplessness, you are arranging things so that it will be even
more difficult for him to change. He learns then that if he
really acts helpless you will break down and do everything
for him. In this way you actually make things much worse.
To be effective in weakening behavior, do not reinforce any
of it. Reinforcing such a behavior only once in a while is
actually a means of making it much stronger (Skinner, 1953).

Earlier it was emphasized that during the initial stages of
strengthening a new behavior it is important to reinforce the
behavior every time it occurs. However, there are two stages
to the training. When the behavior is occurring at the rate

11. reinforcing

16

that you wish—for example, the child dresses himself every day in time for school—then it is important to reinforce him only every other time. If he continues to work on this arrangement, then you would shift to reinforcing him only every third time, then every fourth, and so on until it is necessary to only occasionally comment on the situation. Again, the key word is *gradual*. If his behavior is weakened or disrupted when you reduce the reinforcement, then go back and reinforce him every time for a while. His behavior tells you how fast you can reduce the reinforcement schedule.

When you wish to strengthen behavior, reinforce it every time at first and then gradually lessen the schedule. To weaken a behavior, *never* reinforce it. In the next chapter, we will discuss another means of weakening behavior which is somewhat more complex in the effects it has on all members of the family.

Key Ideas in Chapter 1

Reinforcers strengthen behavior.

Social reinforcers include a smile, a touch, or praise.

Behavior changes are gradual and are most likely to occur if reinforcement is consistent.

Observation and data collection are the first steps in changing behavior.

To weaken a behavior, use nonreinforcement or punishment, or reinforce a replacement behavior.

2

Aversive Stimuli: Variations on a Theme of Punishment

You can change your social environment. Your social environment consists of the people with whom you live. You can change their behavior and they can change yours. One way to change the behavior of another person is to arrange the proper reinforcers for some new behavior. You could also weaken some other behaviors by no longer reinforcing them. These two processes can be used to make gradual but major changes in your immediate social environment.

Sometimes we react as if we believe that behavior must change immediately. When parents punish, they are indicating that things must change right now! Most of us have learned that rapid changes in behavior can sometimes be brought about by using pain or punishment. In fact, some parents become trained to apply it continuously to spouses, children, and anyone else within range. In opting to produce quick changes by using punishment, they pay a price—as we shall presently see.

You Get What You Give

Punishment "works." If you use it properly it will produce rapid changes in the behavior of other people. If this is so, why not use it all of the time, as some people seem to do? The reason why it must be used cautiously is that there is a price tag attached. Observation of real people in real social settings shows that *the individual who gives the most reinforcement receives the most reinforcement and that the person in the family who gives the most punishment receives the most* 1_____ *from other family members. You get what you give.*

There is an odd kind of equity which holds when people interact with each other. We get what we give, both in amount and in kind. Each of us seems to have his own bookkeeping system for love, and for pain. Over time, the books are balanced, as is shown in a number of studies actually observing how people act toward each other (Patterson and Reid, 1970).

If the mother yells and screams at the children, they will find ways of punishing her in return. Studies do show that mothers who yell and scold a lot have children who do the same. In some families the child may pay his mother back by stealing from her purse. The husband who shouts at his wife may find that his meals are poorly prepared.

The price for using aversive stimuli to control behavior is that they will be returned in amount and perhaps in kind. In a family, the person who does the most punishing will receive the 2_____ punishment from others. The whole family can become very busy playing the endless game of "getting even." For this reason, punishment should be used sparingly, if at all.

When people think of punishment occurring in a family, they ordinarily think of scolding, yelling, and spanking because these are the things which occur most often. However, a surprising number of parents use hitting as a means of punishing the child. They wait until the child's behavior is absolutely intolerable and then rush in, hitting to the right and left in a desperate attempt to get things calmed down. In one sense this "works." After the hitting, things are usually

1. punishment   2. most

pretty quiet *for a short time.* The noise and clamor subside. This reinforces the parents for hitting. The next time the children get into a noisy hassle the parents are more likely to resort to hitting again. When the parents scold or hit, the children stop being disruptive for a few minutes, which reinforces the parents for 3_____ or 4_____ . In this manner the children train parents to scold and yell a good part of the day. Parents who scold and hit are not "bad" people or "sick" people. They have simply allowed their 5_____ to train them to do things they really don't want to be doing.

The children's hassling seldom slows down for more than a few moments after a scolding. Many parents find themselves caught up in an endless cycle of the children's fighting, followed by their nagging, with this followed by a brief period of quiet, and then a repetition of the whole episode.

There are some kinds of punishment that do work. But most parents do not make use of them; instead they persist in allowing their children to teach them to use the wrong punishment at the wrong time.

Using Punishment Effectively

Mrs. W is working in the kitchen getting supper ready for her four children. In the next room, the noise level has been steadily building for the past few moments. One of the children runs into the kitchen: "Momma, Sherry took my doll." Sherry comes bouncing into the room laughing, "Your doll is behind the stove." Mrs. W says to the younger sister, "Momma's busy, you go and play. Sherry, you behave yourself." Shortly after the two children leave the room, there is a resounding crash and the young infant breaks into a piercing

3. scolding   4. hitting   5. children

cry. Mrs. W runs into the next room and is greeted with Sherry's shouting, "I didn't do it, Mommy! She fell off the chair!" Without breaking her stride, Mrs. W strikes Sherry, pushing her aside, and runs to her baby. The infant is not seriously injured but now Sherry is crying as well and the mother is shouting at all of the children in the room.

Mrs. W waited too long. There was a five- or ten-minute period in which the children were becoming increasingly out of control. It should have been possible to interfere with the build-up by sending one or more children outside or bringing one of them into the kitchen to help her. By doing either of these things she would be using a *mild* form of punishment (removal from the group) and heading off the trouble before it really began.

In this family, Sherry is the instigator—she indis-criminately teases her sisters, her mother, the dog, the cat, and even her grandmother whenever Grandma has the cour-age to visit. The mother could have applied a mild punish-ment when it became reasonably clear that Sherry was teasing her younger sister. She could have used Time Out (see Chapter 8). Time Out means removing Sherry from all rein-forcement by sending her to the bathroom for five minutes. Mrs. W could also have said, "You were teasing, that means no dessert for you tonight." In this situation there is no scolding; i.e., she did not say, "You are a bad girl," nor did she scream, "Sher-ry! Stop that!"

If you decide to use punishment, *stay calm. Catch the problem at its beginning, then use some mildly aversive natural consequence every time.*

It is amazingly difficult to use a mild consequence 6_____ time the problem behavior occurs. Most of us would simply rather not bother. Do it now. Do it every time. Most parents find that it helps them be consistent in handling such a problem by using the observation and record-

6. every

ing procedures described in Chapter 5. To really change such a behavior you must set aside a week or two in which you carefully track the behavior and consistently react when it occurs. Furthermore, when using even moderate punishments you should increase the amount of reinforcement which the child is receiving for pro-social behavior. For example, you might make it a point to reinforce him for a set of behaviors which would compete with teasing. Each time Mrs. W sees Sherry playing well with one of her sisters, she should go over and say, "Hey, that's really nice. You two are playing so quietly I hardly knew you were here. What are you doing?" A few moments' participation would be a powerful 7_____ for Sherry's playing with her sister. When using mildly punishing consequences to 8_____ a problem behavior, also plan to *use reinforcement to strengthen some set of behaviors that will take its place.*

Changing behavior requires that you have a plan or a program and that you follow it for a week or two. To be consistent in reinforcing some behaviors and ignoring or punishing others, it is necessary to collect and record your observations. Just "making up your mind" is not sufficient for most parents, particularly when they are first learning.

Homework

Count the number of critical comments, scolds, disagreements, lectures, and nags you deliver to one member of the family over a five-day period. Each time one occurs, make a mark on a piece of paper that you keep handy. This kind of record keeping will also alert you to errors in timing. You should begin to notice whether you tend to wait too long and how consistent you are. It will probably turn out that you are a "random nagger," that is, for the same behavior sometimes you nag and sometimes you don't.

7. reinforcer   8. weaken

Key Ideas in Chapter 2

You get what you give:
    to get more reinforcement, give more; and
    to get less punishment, give less.
If you decide to use punishment,
    intervene early;
    use mildly aversive consequences every time;
    remain calm; and
    set up a program to reinforce competing behaviors.

3
Accidental Training: Unplanned Reinforcement

It is a paradox that sometimes *we create reinforcement arrangements that train our close friends, members of our families, and others whom we love to display high rates of problem behaviors.* We also set up reinforcements that strengthen problem behavior in ourselves. Such programs are extremely effective, even though they are unplanned.

Problem Behaviors Are Accidentally Reinforced

"How are you ever going to get to be a big, strong man if you don't eat?" Timmy, a large, corpulent eight-year-old, sits staring down at the plate heaped with food that his mother has placed in front of him. "But I don't really want all that, Ma." "You shouldn't have had a snack when you came home today. When your mama goes to all that work getting a big supper you should eat. Tell him, Herman, that he should eat." With a sigh Timmy picks up his fork. "That's a good boy. Your mama loves you."

When you go to someone's home for dinner there is a good deal of pressure for you to overeat. Aside from praising the food, the primary reinforcer given the cook is your asking for seconds. In order to reinforce him, you overeat. Similarly, in many homes the reinforcer for the mother is to have everyone eat as if they were preparing for a snowshoe trip into the arctic wasteland. The mother reinforces her child for strenuous overeating and then attributes his overweight to the fact that his Uncle Charlie was fat. If he does not overeat, she punishes him. When he stuffs himself, she reinforces him. Many problems of overweight in children are caused by accidental training by well-meaning parents. In the example above, the mother nags until Timmy overeats and then 1_____ him for overeating. This combination of criticism and 2_____ is very effective.

In another kind of home the parents provide social reinforcers for the child's performing as an entertainer. He may be largely ignored unless he behaves like a clown or a buffoon; then his family becomes involved and interested, reinforcing him at a high rate for doing and saying silly things. "Isn't he cute? Look at the way he makes a face. He'll be on TV someday."

When visitors arrive the parents prompt the child to get him started and then reinforce him when he performs. This is not to say that "clown" is a terribly deviant set of behaviors to have in one's list of skills. It becomes a problem if it is his *only* means of turning on his parents or of relating to others. For example, are they as reinforcing to him when he wishes to discuss an idea that he has or a book he has read?

A more typical example of accidental training for problem behaviors is found in the systematic programs for training in helplessness and immaturity. This is such a frequent problem in normal families that programs are described in later chapters for altering these behaviors. There are a number of variations on this theme. In the most common one, the mother reinforces the child when he behaves in a helpless fashion. The father may also punish him for being less than perfect when he does attempt to behave in a grownup manner.

1. reinforces   2. reinforcement

As the father sits down to supper, Scot, the six-year-old, reaches over and takes a piece of bread and begins putting butter on it. The butter is a little hard and doesn't spread well. He begins to whine and his mother interrupts what she was saying to her husband. "Oh, here, let me do it," she says in an exasperated tone. She talks to her husband as she butters Scot's bread and then also cuts the meat on his plate into bite-sized chunks.

Scot whined and acted helpless, so his mother did everything for him. In this situation, when he 3_____ , he was reinforced. Apparently it is easier for Scot's mother to do it for him than to train him to do it for himself. This is a small thing, but repeat this scene in a dozen different settings each day and you have a training program in which a boy is being reinforced for helplessness. If he says that he wants to go down the street half a block to the neighbor's, his mother goes with him. When he has difficulty tying his shoes in the morning, she 4_____ them for him. She does this because she believes it is quicker than taking the time to teach him how to do it for himself.

If Scot does try to tie his shoes, his father is likely to remark, "Look at that kid; he can't even do that right." He is punished for trying to develop skills. He gets reinforced for remaining 5_____ . No chores are arranged for Scot because it is "easier" for the parents to do the chores themselves. The child is seldom given the opportunity for developing skills, and thus gets little support for learning new competencies. As suggested by Ebner (1970), this child is a "trained incompetent."

Many parents like these report that they do not like helpless behaviors. They simply drift into this type of training program because they did not wish to take the time to plan programs for skill training.

3. whined   4. ties   5. helpless

Punishment Behaviors Are Reinforced

The second kind of accidental training is done with pain and punishment; it is equally effective in training adults and children. Typically, the behavior changes slowly enough over time so that neither party is aware of the changes in behavior.

The general principle involved was covered earlier; *whatever turns off something painful is strengthened.* When the TV set is turned up too high and your yelling leads someone to turn it down, then you were reinforced for 6_____ . In effect, yelling "worked"; it reduced the pain. A response that was reinforced is more likely to occur again in the 7_____.

Noise coming from the two younger brothers playing in the living room usually leads to a remark such as "Hey! Stop that fighting in there or you will both get a spanking!" Usually the boys will quiet down for a few minutes. The noise or "pain" is reduced, so you get reinforced for yelling and making threats. If your children are noisy very often, they could teach you to do a lot of yelling. In this situation, the children are training the 8_____ .

Things that make it possible for you to avoid pain are reinforcing. "Forgetting" to keep an appointment with the dentist is reinforcing. Bowling with friends is reinforcing. It could be doubly reinforcing if the family has trained the wife to be a nag. She in turn has trained her husband and children to stay out of the house. There is a paradox here because the family probably does not want her to be a nag and she does not really want her husband or children to be out of the home so much. However, the wife drifts into nagging and the husband drifts into staying away from home. Both behaviors "work" in terms of temporarily shutting off painful stimuli.

Children are involved in similar ways. If the younger sister has a comic that her brothers want to look at, they may ask for it; if she refuses, they may simply hit her and take it away. In this instance hitting and taking are reinforced be-

6. yelling   7. future   8. parents

28

cause they "work." The child learns that he doesn't have to wait; whenever some other member of the family presents him with a minor pain such as teasing, yelling, or noncompliance, he can turn them off immediately by hitting. He gets paid off for hitting.

If parents do not carefully track teasing and hitting, it is very easy for one or more of the children to learn to become a first-class monster. This kind of training goes on frequently in many homes (Patterson and Reid, 1970) and nursery schools (Bandura and Walters, 1963). In this kind of accidental training, the victim's response to being hit provides the 9_____ that strengthens the hitting behavior. Nagging works because it temporarily reduces the noise; hitting is reinforced because it helps the hitter change things which are unpleasant for him. He doesn't have to learn how to teach his little brother to make less noise; he can hit him and turn it off immediately. He doesn't have to do chores; his temper tantrums will teach his 10_____ to stop asking him to do things.

In a great many of the families with whom we have worked, *all* of the members spend a great deal of time yelling, hitting, and punishing each other. In fact, observations in homes suggest that many otherwise quite normal families drift into patterns of this type.

You are responsible for the social environment in which you live. If you don't like it, then 11_____ it. If there are some things about it that you like, then begin tracking what other people are doing that please you and 12_____ them when those actions occur. Do not take good things for granted, and do not feel that you have to put up with annoying or unpleasant behaviors either. It's your world. Observe it. And observe yourself to see what it is you are doing that makes it the way it is.

9. reinforcement   10. parents   11. change   12. reinforce

Key Ideas in Chapter 3

It is easy to accidentally reinforce problem behaviors.

Punishment behaviors, such as nagging, scolding, and hitting, that turn off painful behaviors are strengthened.

You make your own social environment.

Section II
BEHAVIOR MANAGEMENT SKILLS

The previous section on social learning gave some general notions on how behavior can be changed. It is not, of course, a complete theory of human behavior, but we don't think that a theory has to be able to explain everything in order for it to be useful. As the theory stands right now, we *can* use it to change much of our social environment.

Understanding general notions or principles is not enough. It is also necessary to understand and practice the procedures for putting these notions to work. This next section outlines the practical skills that must be mastered before you can be effective in changing behavior; we call these procedures "behavior management skills." We now move from theory to practice.

The ideas about how to make these principles work have evolved gradually as a result of our years of experience in working with families who are having problems. As the parents tried to put these social learning principles into practice, certain difficulties were encountered. The efforts of numerous investigators to meet such difficulties led to the development of what might now be called "behavior management skills." In retrospect, these skills can be found in many well-run homes and nursery schools that are managed by

33

adults who do these things quite naturally. In some respects, the contribution of the last decade's work may amount to little more than underlining what it was that some parents did that was so effective in teaching their children. Observation data collected in the families in the last decade helped us to understand which of these practices are crucial to good child management and which are not.

Parents can learn these skills and use them in child management and in settling differences between adult members of the family. However, it would be wishful thinking to believe that merely reading about these procedures could change longstanding severe problems. The reader is urged to supplement careful study of the chapters in Section II with aid and supervision from a trained behavior modifier when actually implementing a program in behavior change.

4

How to Do It:
Precision Reinforcement

The ability to use social reinforcers to change behavior is a skill possessed by very few people, and one that is somewhat analogous to skill in using the English language. Everyone does it hundreds of times each day, but few of us do it well. Your ability to help your child change his behavior, and have the change persist, will depend largely upon your ability to practice the skills outlined in this chapter. None of the ideas presented here will be unfamiliar to you. Not one of the ideas is too complicated for a five-year-old child to understand. However, most people put these ideas into practice so haphazardly that they come to feel that it is impossible to change the behavior of other people.

Reinforce Immediately and Often

The first concept to be emphasized is that when you see a behavior that you like, reinforce it. Many parents notice when the child does something which they especially like, but say that if they indicate their approval it will "spoil" the child. This is probably just an excuse. Such a "sphinx parent" seldom reinforces anyone. He believes that the child ought to behave because that is what children are supposed to do. In our experience, sphinx parents can change and thus become more effective parents.

At the other extreme is the "gusher," who hugs, caresses, praises, and attends no matter what the child does. It is not that he "loves too much," but that he 1_____ the child no matter what he does. A good behavior manager reinforces immediately when desirable behavior occurs. *If* the child behaves, *then* reinforce him. If not, then ignore the behavior. Ignoring the behavior over a long period of time will 2_____ it.

Parents often want to teach the child to do something regularly that he does only once in a while. For example, many parents complain, "He almost never talks to us."

Harold comes in from school, and walks into the kitchen. He says, "Hi, Mom," and peers into the refrigerator. His mother, in the middle of preparing supper, hardly looks up as she says, "How was it today?" He stands looking at a magazine, absent-mindedly leafing through it as he munches. "We had a race at school today for some guys who came to see how fast we were." Mother, by now deep in her casserole, says, from a great distance, "That's nice." Harold goes into the other room.

Actually, Harold won that race and was the fastest runner in the third grade, as his mother discovered later. He could have said that he had won an Olympic gold medal and still received only a mumbled "That's nice" as a reinforcer. The point is that he talked and she did 3_____ reinforce him effectively. If you occasionally miss supporting a pro-social behavior, it is no great matter. But if you miss all of the time, then your Harold will simply stop giving you that behavior.

Reinforcing Harold would require only that his mother listen to him attentively for a few moments and ask him

1. reinforces   2. weaken   3. not

about his race. She might actually stop working for a few moments but that is probably not necessary. What *is* required is that she listen carefully to what he is saying. When he talks, she 4_____ . In doing this, she is providing the immediate reinforcement required to strengthen a behavior. If she reinforces him in this way for talking about school, he will, in the future, be more likely to 5_____ . During the early stages of training she should reinforce him 6_____ time he attempts to describe things going on in his life.

Thus far we have made two points. *To strengthen a behavior, reinforce it* 7_____ *and reinforce it* 8_____ *time.* Even after the child has learned to regularly engage in the new behavior, you should never take the behavior for granted. If you like what he is doing, 9_____ him for it.

It would be difficult to overemphasize the importance of reinforcing *immediately*. The longer you wait, the less likely it is to be effective. For example, one mother waits until after supper to tell her daughter that she appreciated her hanging up her coat. A second parent reinforces her son a few seconds after he hangs up his coat. The child most likely to hang up his coat in the future would be the one who was reinforced 10_____ . Don't wait. Do it now.

Reinforce Small Steps Toward the Goal

If the words "immediate" and "often" summarize the first two points made in this chapter, the phrase "small steps" would best characterize the third. How do you really teach a child to "be a good student," to "talk to me," to "be more polite," or to "be more assertive"? If you were to wait until your child gets all B's on his report card to reinforce him, it would never happen. This is a very complex behavior with literally hundreds of small steps required to reach a goal. But

4. listens   5. talk   6. every   7. immediately
8. every   9. reinforce   10. immediately

those small steps are the points along the way where you can reinforce him. If you plan to wait until he is President of the United States before you reinforce him, he may not even learn to tie his shoes.

Some parents behave as if using reinforcers "wears them out," or as if it will spoil the child. It isn't too much love that spoils a child; it is being reinforced for the wrong behaviors.

Reinforce him for starting and then for each step along the way. This process is called "shaping." It consists of two steps. First *decide just what it is that you wish to bring about.* Second, *decide on the steps necessary to arrive at this point and break them down into very small and specific units.* Let's take as an example the goal of "being a good student" for a boy who consistently earns less than a D average. The teachers say that he could do much better work. What kind of grades would it be reasonable to aim for as a goal for your training program?

Begin with a rather modest goal of, say, a C average. Next, think of just what your child would have to do to earn a C average, for example, completing more of his homework assignments. Maybe he should begin studying early in the term; perhaps he needs a consistent study program. These are vague goals, though, and they do not constitute a description of a program.

If an average child studies one hour a day, five days a week, at the start of the term, he should be able to earn at least a C average. Now that you have a specific goal, teach him to study an hour a day. Notice, the word is "teach," not "force." Next, you must decide where and when the training will take place. Select a quiet place in your home, perhaps his room, where he is to study. Then, after discussing it with him, set a time most convenient for him and the rest of the family; for example, right after supper and before the TV set is turned on is often a good time.

A good student may study an hour a day. However, for someone who does not study at all, an hour a day is an enormous step. If he tries it, it will almost certainly be painful to him and he probably will not use the time well. Take a smaller step. In fact, begin where he is now. If he actually studies about five minutes a day, begin there.

On the first day, he studies five minutes in his room and then he gets reinforced. Do not test him to find out if he really studied. For some children, just sitting still for five minutes might be an adequate first step.

The reinforcer may be praise from you. Or perhaps he must study five minutes to earn a natural consequence, such as the right to watch TV that night: no studying, no TV. There are many kinds of reinforcers that could be used (see Chapter 7). It is important that *your program begins where the child's skills are.* Set up the beginning of the program so that he is almost certain to earn a 11_____. Gradually increase the size of the steps. After the second or third day you might set the study timer (a kitchen timer will do) at ten minutes. Increase the steps only when you are reasonably sure that he can stay in there and work for that period of time. If ten minutes is too long, then go back to five minutes for a while. Keep the steps within his range.

If your program breaks down, then your steps are too 12_____. It may also be that the reinforcers are too weak. Change your program. If he stops studying it does not mean that he is a bad boy or a "hopeless case." It simply means that you have to change the 13_____.

Use of Punishment and Bribes

As he goes along, increase the requirements so that he must do more work in order to earn the same reinforcers. By the end of a week or two he may be studying fifteen or twenty minutes each evening. For some children, talking to him about his work is a powerful reinforcer. That does not mean a quiz session in which you try to decide whether he really knows the material. Do not nag him about his work. *Do not punish him for performance that is less than perfect.* Rather,

11. reinforcer   12. large   13. program

your role is to reinforce him for slow gradual development of skills that will lead to a C grade.

Bill comes out of his room after his study session and puts his books on the kitchen table. His father looks up from reading the paper. "There is the clock watcher now. How did it go?" Bill just replies, "OK," as he goes toward the TV set. The father has put down his paper. "Well, how about letting me take a look at what you have been doing?" Bill looks dejected; apparently he has been through this many times before. The father takes the essay that Bill was working on. "Get this all done tonight?" Bill nods. "This sure is messy. Why don't you use an eraser? Hey, what kind of spelling do they teach you kids nowadays? How do you spell . . . ." And the inquisition goes on. . . and on. . . .

This is not a good example of a parent reinforcing a child for the first steps in a study program. Rather, it is a good example of a father using 14_____ for behaviors that fail to be perfect. Bill doesn't have to become President in order to earn a reinforcer.

The result of such a training program will be that Bill simply stops engaging in the study behavior at all. The father will report that he used small steps and social reinforcers but the program did not work. The error lay in the father's use of 15_____ . Punishment almost always 16_____ the response that it follows. This father, in his role of "prosecuting attorney," is training the boy to 17_____ studying. He is actually working against the goal which he has set—to help his son study.

One alternative to all of this emphasis upon specific goals, small steps, lots of reinforcement, and no punishment is to offer a bribe. A bribe usually means offering a large reward to get someone to do something that is illegal. There is another sense in which some parents use a bribe. This parent seldom reinforces pro-social behaviors; therefore his

14. punishment   15. punishment   16. weakens   17. stop

training programs for the child have been so sloppy that he can't be sure of what the child is going to do next. So he uses a bribe: "If you are a good boy and don't tease or fight for the whole week that your grandmother is here, we will give you a dollar." There is nothing illegal about it. The under-achieving student is often bribed: "I'll give you five dollars for every A that you get," or "I'll give you a dollar for every C that you get." The problem with using bribes is simply that these kinds of bribes often do not work. As used by most parents, bribes are an inept use of a reward to cover up the fact that they have done a sloppy job of training the child.

In the example above, the child was told that he would be reinforced for studying, or for being good. *That* is good. He was also told the specific goal is for him to get an A or a C or to play with his sister without teasing and fighting. Those goals were somewhat vague. Practically speaking, the pro-grams were sloppy because, for many children, the steps required to reach the goal were too large and/or not clearly specified. *How* do you get an A, anyway?

The child might work out a study program on his own, but why leave things to chance? If the child does happen to work out a study program, would the parent-briber remem-ber to reinforce him each day for making a step at a time? Probably not; such a parent would feel that it is easier to dole out the five dollars at the end of the whole series of steps. Parents who use bribes don't have to feel responsible; they can always say that they "tried." If the bribe fails, it is the child's fault; the parent "did his duty." *The bribe is usually a substitute for the parents' planning a program and participat-ing in it every day.* If the child's behavior is important, it deserves your careful planning and participation. Anything worth doing deserves something better than a bribe.

If a planned program does not work, any one of three things may be involved. The 18 _____ may be too large, the 19 _____ may be too weak, or you might be mixing in a good deal of 20 _____ while you reinforce the child. Sit down and talk to the child about what you are

18. steps   19. reinforcer   20. punishment

trying to do and let him help you design a better program. *If the child's behavior is not changing, it is not his fault; it is just a bad program.* Keep changing it until it works.

Precision Reinforcement: An Example

The concept of shaping is so crucial that it might be helpful to work through one more example. This time we will work with the problem of thumb-sucking in a four-year-old child. After observing that during the hour before bedtime he has his thumb in his mouth an average of about thirty-five minutes, the parents have planned a program. Their observations show that he is fairly consistent over two or three days. They are now ready to begin a program; they give him the following explanation.

"Tim, you say you want to stop sucking your thumb. It does seem hard for you to stop. Well, we are going to help you practice not sucking your thumb. I think it will be fun for you. Practice time will be just before you go to bed. If you can go for five minutes without putting your thumb in your mouth, you get to put a mark here on this card on the refrigerator. When you get ten marks, you and I will take a special trip to the zoo, just for you. I will set the kitchen timer so we will know when five minutes have gone by. Let's practice now to see how this works. Ready? Remember, do not put your thumb in your mouth and you earn one mark."

The instructions should be clear, specific, and with the least amount of implied criticism or subtle nagging. Emphasize that it will be fun for him, as indeed it will when it comes time to put the mark on his chart on the refrigerator. If he is not successful on the first trial, label the behavior for him. "Oh, oh. You forgot and put it in your mouth. Let's try again, you goofed that one." Reset the timer but do not nag or scold. Keep the learning situation as pleasant and reinforcing as you can. When he goes the whole five minutes, then reinforce him: "Hey, you made it that time. No thumb in the mouth at all. That is really big boy stuff. Let's put a mark on your chart." If he then goes on and gets another five-minute block, you might increase the time interval to seven or eight minutes.

Mention your pleasure at his successful practice at other times during the day. One of the best reinforcers is to "brag" about him when a friend drops by and he happens to be in earshot. "Tim is really working on not sucking his thumb; today he went for almost a whole hour without sucking his thumb even once. He is really becoming a big boy."

If you notice at any time during the day that he does not have his thumb in his mouth, you should reinforce him. "Hey, there is no thumb in your mouth." Announce his successes at the family dinner table and encourage the other members to reinforce him. These programs are all-out efforts and for best results should involve as many members of the family as possible.

Each day the time intervals should be increased so that eventually his step is a full hour to earn one mark. You might then increase the time interval to several hours. At the end of two to three weeks, the effects should carry over to other times of the day and the program could be gradually phased out. This means that the time required to earn a mark has become large (a day); by this time the marks themselves may have become reinforcers. Later, when you think he is ready, ask him if he thinks you could drop the record keeping. He may decide to keep his own records. If his progress is maintained, you then might also consider reducing your schedule of marks and use only social reinforcers. However, to be maintained, his behavior must be 21＿＿＿＿＿ once in a while.

The thumb-sucking is likely to recur from time to time, for example, when grandmother comes to visit. You might

21. reinforced

then explain the program to her and use some sections of it for a day or two. Programs are family affairs. Simply re-introduce some, or all, of the old program until the behavior disappears again.

In summary, discuss with the child what it is that you are trying to do. Tell him you are going to work together on a problem that has been difficult for him to handle. Use as little 22_____ as possible. Have a specific goal in mind. Begin the program at such a level that he is bound to receive an immediate 23_____ .

As he moves along, increase the size of the steps. If at all possible, involve several members of the 24_____ as reinforcers (not as spies). When the behavior is under control, gradually fade out the program. Be prepared for an occasional return of the old problem behavior.

Homework

For a three-day period record the number of social rein-forcers you use with your children. Select a one-hour period—the same one each day, for example, five to six p.m. Record on paper the total for each day.

After this baseline period, practice each day for a week doubling the number of reinforcers. Keep a record each day. This may seem very artificial at first, but after a few days of practice it will become quite natural. Your skill as a social reinforcer is one of the keys to the success of the programs you introduce. Touch your children and spouse, kiss them or praise them. Try to make the reinforcers contingent upon behaviors that you particularly value.

22. punishment   23. reinforcer   24. family

Key Ideas in Chapter 4

To strengthen a behavior, reinforce it immediately and do it every time.

To set up a program,
>   decide on a specific goal;
>   assess where the child is now in relation to that goal; and
>   use small and specific steps to achieve the goal.

Do not punish performance that is less than perfect.

Bribing is *not* a behavior change program.

If the behavior does not change, it is a bad program, not a bad child.

5

First Steps in Setting Up a Management Program

Review: Principles of Reinforcement

This section is a brief review of the key notions scattered throughout the previous chapters. These concepts are related directly to the application of behavior management skills.

When considering a training program, remember to keep track of and plan for the changes in *two* responses. One response is the problem behavior that you wish to weaken. The other is the pro-social behavior that will take its place. *Arrange a program that will* 1_____ *the problem behavior and* 2_____ *the pro-social behavior.*

First 3_____ and count each of the behaviors. Notice the reinforcing arrangements for each that exist within the family.

Second, plan a program that specifies the goal you wish to achieve.

Third, specify the steps required to get there. A good program will lay out the small steps required to achieve the goal; it will also include the reinforcers needed to strengthen the new behaviors. During the early stages of the program

1. weaken   2. strengthen   3. observe

4_____ small step is reinforced 5_____.
The program should also spell out the arrangements used to weaken the problem behavior. These arrangements, if used at all, should stress nonreinforcement or Time Out as the principal means of weakening behavior. Do not use physical 6_____ , nagging, or criticism.

Behaviors do not change in one day or even in one week. It may take several weeks before behavior changes show in the data. The observation data help you to keep track of just what the changes are; if they show that the behavior hasn't altered, then change the program. The steps may be too large; the reinforcers may be too 7_____ or too few. Perhaps you are not being consistent: Some problem behaviors may get reinforced. Perhaps you are not giving social reinforcers or points every time the new behaviors occur. Perhaps you mix your arrangements so that the child is receiving both positive reinforcers and punishment for the new behaviors. If the child's behavior does not change, it means that you and your program must change.

You should plan on involving other family members in the program. However, it is important to structure their roles not as spies, but rather as positive reinforcers. The only type of data that you should allow a sibling to bring you is something that indicates your child has just earned a positive reinforcer.

"Jane is trying to remember to wash her face when she comes to the table. It is really a hard thing to remember, so you can help her by telling her whenever you notice how clean her face is at breakfast or supper. When she forgets, don't say anything. No nagging, right?"

The social learning approach assumes that you are responsible for your own behavior and for that of the people

4. every   5. immediately   6. punishment   7. weak

in close contact with you. You can change your social environment; you can also make arrangements for changing your own behavior.

Observing, Counting, and Recording

On the face of it, observing and counting just do not seem to be the kind of things you do when you wish to help someone. Behavior can, of course, be changed without anyone carrying out these activities. However, strange as it may seem at first, you are more likely to be successful if you take the additional time and care involved to observe and to count. Certainly, the improvements in your own behavior or in that of your child are important enough—they are worth the five or ten minutes of your time required each day for these activities.

Observing and counting the behaviors may bring an interesting bonus, first noted by Lindsley (1970). The simple act of counting the occurrences of some of your own behaviors can change their rate of occurrence! For example, if you wish to increase time spent reading, you might begin to count the number of minutes spent reading each day. For some people, the act of observing and recording produces increases in reading. On the other hand, if you were interested in reducing fingernail-biting or angry thoughts about your spouse, daily recordings of these behaviors could produce decreases in their occurrence. In a sense, careful observation and record keeping give you better control over your own behavior.

Most of us do not observe either ourselves or anyone else very carefully. A curious fact pointed out by the Lindsley investigators is that calmly recording the incidence of a behavior occurring in the spouse or the child can serve to reduce the incidence of problem behaviors. Each time the child teases his sister, calmly state, "There is another one," as you record the event on a chart located on the refrigerator door. This is likely to produce a 8_____ in rate. Such reductions may, of course, be short-lived unless you also provide increased social reinforcers for the pro-social behavior that takes its place.

Aside from these bonus effects, another reason for collecting observation data lies in the fact that behavior usually changes slowly. If you have spent the required ten minutes a day observing and counting, then you can see that over time there has been a slow but perceptible decrease in the problem behavior. Without the data you might become discouraged and either change the program unnecessarily or give up altogether. Some behavior changes may require several weeks. The daily sessions of collecting data serve as excellent reminders to carry out the rest of the program.

Get in the habit of collecting data on everything about your social environment that is of interest to you. Most professional behavior modifiers collect data on themselves and their loved ones. We do this, not because we "love science," but simply because it makes it possible to aid people we care about very much. Some also keep daily records on up to eight or ten of their own behaviors. Altogether such extensive record keeping requires but a few minutes each day.

Pinpointing the Problem Behavior

To be able to observe, you must first be able to *pinpoint the behavior you are attempting to control.* Pinpointing means being specific. What is it that you wish to change? "He is just mean all the time" is *not* pinpointing the problem; the statement is much too vague. Specifically, what is it that he does that leads you to describe him as mean? As you watch him more carefully, you might note that he hits others, breaks their toys, says cruel things, and talks back to his parents. These are all countable behaviors. If you can't count the behavior, you have not pinpointed it properly.

8. reduction

50

Take the statement "He is an immature child." How would you count that? Parents who complain about this problem usually go on to describe any one or all of the following. "He makes us do things for him that he can really do for himself, he talks baby talk, he whines, he cries all of the time, he will not play with other children but hangs onto his mother all day." The list of specific behaviors describing one immature child would not necessarily describe another. Each family must construct their own list.

In pinpointing your first problem, try to select one that occurs about five or more times a day. For example, teasing is a behavior which often fulfills this requirement. To pinpoint it for your child, first observe for a few days to see what it is that he does; write these behaviors down on a list. Tape the list to the refrigerator door where both of you can see it. You should also pinpoint its opposite. Specifically, what is it that you wish the child would do instead of tease? You might make a list of these behaviors, such as "play quietly with his brother," "sit and watch TV without fighting," and "share things." You can set up two places on your daily data chart: one for "teases" and one for "pro-social." Once you agree on these specifics, then establish a baseline.

Establishing a Baseline

To establish a baseline you observe and count behaviors for at least three or four days. Do not use a program at this time. Both parents should count the behaviors each day. If the behavior occurs more than once an hour, you can obtain a stable picture of what is going on by just observing for an hour or two each day.

The mother could observe during the morning and afternoon. The father could begin recording when he comes home from work and might continue until the child goes to bed. Each time the behavior occurs, make a mark on the data chart. If the response lasts more than one minute you might mark it more than once, up to five times if necessary. Both parents should participate in observing and collecting data.

Your baseline observations should cover at least three or four 9_____ . Compare notes and talk about what you are seeing. You should begin to get a much better understanding of this behavior. Particularly notice the reinforcers that keep it going. Most children will be curious about what this is all about. When they ask, tell them; be brief and as nonpunishing as possible.

"Mom, what is that junk on the refrigerator for, anyway? Are you counting me or what?" Mrs. J continued setting the table and said in a matter-of-fact voice, "Well, you know how much trouble you and Lari have with the teasing. Neither one of you seems to be able to stop it, so we thought we would try to help. Right now we are just counting each tease. Later we will do some things that will help you practice not teasing. I think if we all work together, we can change that and it will be better for everyone. By the way, once we start practicing the new thing, it should be fun for you and for Lari."

He may object to being counted and have a temper tantrum right on the spot. Ignore it. If you cannot ignore it, walk out of the room. Do not get involved in long debates with the child as to whether you have the right to observe and count his behavior. You are the parent and you *do* have the right. You may give the child a brief, calm description of what you are doing and why you are doing it. Do not 10_____ .

It is helpful for recording behaviors to wear a counter on your wrist. The most efficient piece of equipment seems to be a golfer's counter that can be bought for prices ranging from three to six dollars. Whether using a pencil and paper or a wrist counter, record your data each day on a data card.

9. days   10. debate

52

The chart which we have found useful looks like this; you can easily make your own or use one of those provided at the back of this book.

```
┌─────────────────────────────────────────────────────────────┐
│                      DATA CARD                               │
│                                                              │
│   Name   Scot                                                │
│                                                              │
│   Behavior:  Swearing: says H-d,  s-,  s-o-b,                │
│                    and  b-.                                  │
│                                                              │
│           Number of            Time                          │
│   Day     Behaviors          Interval           Rate         │
│                                                              │
│ 2/11 Mon   MH I       8:30 a.m. - 4 p.m.      .8/hr.         │
│                                                              │
│ 2/12 Tues MH MH IIII  8:30 a.m. - 10 p.m.    1.03/hr.       │
│                                                              │
│                                                              │
│                                                              │
└─────────────────────────────────────────────────────────────┘
```

Post this where everyone can see it. Each time an event occurs, label it: "That was a swear." Record it, and *let it go:* no lectures, no nagging. At the end of the day add up the number of minutes or hours during which you observed, and divide that into the number of behaviors you observed; put the resulting figure into the column labeled "rate." This makes it possible to compare a day when you only observed four hours to one on which you observed sixteen hours.

In summary, then, first pinpoint the behavior by drawing up a list of 11_____ behaviors that define the problem. Agree upon a time during which you will count. Record 12_____ event on the data chart or wrist

11. specific   12. each

counter. Record the time during which the observations were made. At the end of the day, calculate the rate by dividing the number of hours (or minutes) into the 13_____ of times the behavior occurred. This gives you an estimate of 14_____. Keep this kind of data for three or four days.

You will find that there are ups and downs. The child may have a good day and then several bad days. When you begin counting, he may have two or even three good days. If so, extend the baseline and continue counting to be sure that it is not just a honeymoon period.

Collecting Data During the Program

After you introduce programs to change the behavior, continue counting. Some programs go on for long periods of time, so it might be a good idea to graph the data so you can get a picture of what is happening. Just looking at a page of numbers can be very confusing. Putting the same material on graph paper helps to clarify basic trends in your program. Several blank sheets of graph paper are included at the back of this book.

Let's suppose that the average rate of swearing for a three-day baseline followed by a week's intervention was: .80; 1.03; .98; 1.20; .80; .89; .70; .90; .60; .65. What do you make of all these numbers? A graph can give you an overall picture at a glance. To prepare a graph, first label each column on the graph paper as a day. The rates for swearing for this boy went to a high point of 1.20, so that could be the top number. Set the bottom number at 0. Count each line between as .10. The first row is .00, the next is .10, the third row is .20, and so forth up to 1.20.

On the following graph (15), put in the rest of the numbers for the rows. The first day of the baseline was Monday, during which time Scot swore .80 times per hour. On

13. number   14. rate

Tuesday, the second day, he swore 1.03 times per hour; enter that on the graph. Now put in the data for the remaining days, given above. It helps in looking at the graph to connect the dots.

15

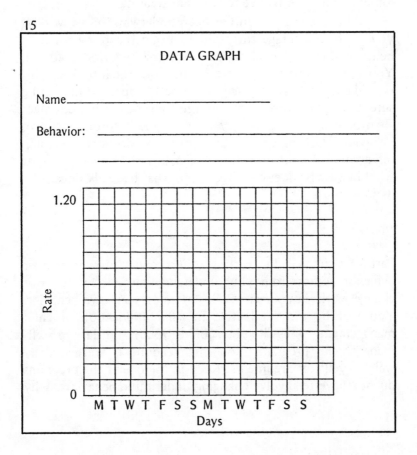

DATA GRAPH

Name_____

Behavior: _____

_____

Rate

1.20

0

M T W T F S S M T W T F S S

Days

In examining the data for this treatment program, it seems that there is a gradual downward slope. Scot seems to be improving. Most of the improvement occurred on the last two days, which were 16_____ and 17_____ . While there is some progress, it does seem to be a weak

15. (Next page)   16. Tuesday   17. Wednesday

program. Continue the program for another two or three days; if the swearing doesn't decrease further, then the program should be changed. Perhaps increasing the reinforcement for not swearing would help; we might also do something more effective to weaken swearing.

After your program has been underway for a few days you might encourage the child to begin recording when he believes the pro-social and/or problem behavior occurred. You might construct a chart for him on which he keeps his own data. At first, it might be wise to supervise him to be sure that you both agree on the behavior being counted. Reinforce him for correctly labeling and recording his own behavior. These procedures amount to the first steps in teaching a child to control his own behavior. Make very sure that what he says he does corresponds to what he really does.

Homework

Part of your skill in assisting other people to change their behavior comes from your understanding of how behavior change works in yourself. Collect data on your own behavior. You will be more effective in your application of child management skills if you could, *today*, initiate a self-management program. You might count cigarettes, daily weight, yells, or arguments. Keep in mind that the programs do not have to involve changing undesirable behaviors. Why

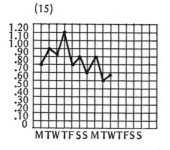

not pinpoint one of your behaviors that you wish to accelerate? For example, suppose you wish to increase the amount of time you spend on one of your hobbies, such as woodworking, painting, or writing. Begin by counting the number of minutes each day that you spend actually engaging in that activity. Post a data chart or a graph in a prominent place, where you will notice it several times each day. Immediately after you have read, painted, or worked in the shop, post your time for that day on the chart.

Remember to keep your initial steps 18_____. Do not try to put in several hours the first day. Put in fifteen or twenty minutes and stop when it becomes even slightly unpleasant. Again, your program for self-control will probably work best if you arrange a specific time and place for the activity. Have a room or a corner in the basement where you keep your materials and try to arrange to use them at the same time each day. Doing this plus recording data will very likely give you some control over your behavior.

Key Ideas in Chapter 5

A program in behavior change should
> weaken the problem behavior, and
> strengthen a pro-social behavior.

Pinpoint specific problem behaviors.

Establish a baseline by observing behaviors for three or four days.

Continue to collect data to chart the progress of your program.

18. small

6

Contracts

"Contracts" is an odd, almost unfriendly word to use when discussing better ways of getting along with other people. However, we have found the concept of contracting indispensable in helping adults get along better with each other. *"Contracts" means writing down the specific behaviors and the reinforcing arrangements that are agreed upon by the persons involved.* Writing such an agreement is a means of being specific, and it is also a commitment: A written agreement is likely to be brought out many times to solve disputes about what someone *really* said in the original agreement.

Just as a rule of thumb, *the older the persons involved, the more important it is that the agreement be negotiated by both parties.* In attempting to work out behavior change agreements with adolescents or spouses, negotiation is mandatory. There are several investigators who have written about the use of contracts (Homme, 1970; Stuart, 1969; Phillips and Wolf, 1968).

Contracting with Younger Children

It seems to be easiest to negotiate with the younger child because generally these contracts only involve a single problem. The parents specify the problem behaviors and the pro-social behaviors which will replace them. After explaining the idea of the program to the child, ask him to select the back-up reinforcer.

"Okay, Jim, each time you come right home after school, you earn points. If you are home at 4:00, you get three points. At 4:30 you get two points, and at 5:00 you get one point. Any later than that, and you have to do dishes that night.

Name _Jim_

Behavior: _Coming home after school_

	M	T	W	T	F	S	S
1st week	3	2	0	3	3		
2nd week	3						
3rd week							
4th week							

Consequences: _Home by 4:00 – 3 pts. Home by 4:30 – 2 pts. Home by 5:00 – 1 pt. Later than 5:00, Jim does the dishes. 10 pts. means a new car for set._

"You could earn fifteen points this week. What would you like to earn for ten points?" Jim still acts as if he is being scolded (the usual thing in his house) and stands staring at the floor. His mother comments, "When you earn fifteen points, you could take the whole family to the pizza parlor, and you decide what we order." Jim looks more interested as his father suggests, "How about ten points means you and I go fishing Sunday afternoon on the McKenzie?" Jim finally says, "Could I get a new car set?" The mother waits for another suggestion and, when none is forthcoming, says, "Well, no, that is a little too expensive. How about for this first week just earning a new car for the set you have? Maybe later on we could talk about a whole new set. Is there anything else you would like to work for?" "No, the car is okay."

Following the discussion, the contract is taped to the refrigerator door.

To conduct a successful program it is necessary to use 1_____ reinforcers as well as the points. Mention each day how well he is doing; brag about his improvements to your friends.

For the first agreement, keep the step small. He should earn his first back-up reinforcer in a week or less. If he is a young child, the time interval might be only a day or two. Do not pay off for "almost" performance; see that he really earns what he gets but try to set the initial step so that he is almost certain to earn his back-up reinforcer.

After he has earned his first back-up reinforcer, he may select a different one for the next step. Give him suggestions if he needs them, but try to respond to what it is that he wants to do.

It need not involve buying him things. Sometimes children enjoy working for things just because they would be fun. For example, they might get to sit in the father's chair at supper, or they might get to decide what desserts the family

1. social

eats for a week. Most children seem to particularly enjoy earning their parents' time. Getting mother for a morning in the park, or father for an afternoon at a movie theater are powerful reinforcers for many children.

Contracting with Older Children and Adolescents

There is a somewhat more complex contract that is useful with the older child (six through adolescence). It is introduced only after the child has already been involved in one or two programs so that he has some general idea of how they work. First, construct a list of problems that occur each day. These are generally things that the child neglects to do. They are presented to the child in such a way that he earns points for "doing the right thing." The list particularly emphasizes the positive things that you wish him to do rather than being a list of "sins." For example:

Name _Dana_							
Behavior (points possible)	M	T	W	T	F	S	S
Brush teeth (1)	1	1					
Make bed (1)	1						
Clean up room (1)	1	1					
Greet people (1)		1					
Get to school on time (1)	1	1					
Do homework (1)		1					
Help with dishes (1)	1	1					
Total	5	6					
Consequences: When Dana has 25 pts., she can have Cynthia spend the night.							

It is a good idea to record the points immediately after the behavior occurs. When you give the child a mark, accompany it with a 2_____ _____. Do not give lectures about the behaviors which did not occur. Simply indicate that "You forgot to brush your teeth, so no points for that."

The advantage of using this checklist is that you can simultaneously strengthen a whole set of behaviors that occur sometimes but are still relatively weak and unpredictable. It saves you the necessity of carrying out a series of six or seven programs.

The idea of the checklist can be extended to cover situations where you are not present, for example, at school, time spent with the baby sitter, or weekends with the grandparents. In these situations the contract must, of course, be negotiated with the child and with the adults who are immediately present in the situations, such as the teacher, the baby sitter, or the grandparents. Typically they will have some idea from previous experience with the child as to the kind of problems they will encounter and which pro-social behaviors need to be strengthened.

The checklist below was constructed for a child who displayed a wide range of out-of-control behaviors. The contract stipulated that the parents provide consequences for behaviors that occur in school. The mother called the teacher each day in order to get the specific information. This cooperation between parents and teacher brought the behaviors under control in relatively short order. The child's world suddenly became quite predictable in terms of providing payoffs for adaptive child behaviors; it also provided for mild but fair punishment for problem behaviors. The child is always aware of what is on the checklist. He helps set the price for each item, sees the results each day, and negotiates the back-up reinforcers for the points. The contract will be changed from time to time, as will be the 3_____-_____ reinforcers.

2. social reinforcer   3. back-up

Name	Dave						
Behavior (points possible)	M	T	W	T	F	S	S
Gets to school on time (2)	2						
Doesn't roam around room (1)	0						
Minds teachers (5)	3						
Gets along w/ other kids (5)	1						
Completes homework (5)	2						
Work is accurate (5)	3						
Behaves on school bus (2)	2						
Gets along w/ brothers (3)	0						
Total	13						

Consequences: 23+ pts. – no chores, picks TV shows
18 – 22 pts. – no TV
13 – 17 pts. – no TV, wash dishes
12 or less – no TV, wash dishes, grounded for 2 days

When working with several settings like this, you should be prepared for repeated changes in the contract toward developing one that really fits the situation. If you are strengthening a large number of behaviors, you should plan on continuing the use of the contracts for several weeks or months.

Graphing the weekly point totals will help chart progress in the program. When you believe the behaviors are under control, you might begin collecting data every other day. If things continue to look good, collect data only once a week. The child's behavior will tell you if you are moving too fast. If your steps are too large, then you will lose control of the 4_____. If this happens, just go back and make the steps 5_____, then increase the value of the 6_____-_____ _____, or use more social reinforcement.

Like collecting data, writing down agreements can become a habit and is probably a good one to acquire. For example, the simple matter of recording on the wall calendar the initials of the children who "did dishes" requires little time, but saves much debating: "I did them two weeks ago!" "No, I did!"

Writing down even such a simple agreement as the following can save many arguments.

Craig can use the car, when it is available, on week nights, but must be in by 10:30. On weekends he can keep it out until 12:30 on one night. He pays for all the gas for any trips out of town. He pays for the insurance. In case of accidents, he pays for repairs. If he gets in later than the agreement allows, he loses the car for one week for each hour that he is late.

This agreement was arrived at only after a good deal of discussion with Craig. It was also changed several times as new problems came up and were discussed. The agreement was not "handed down" by the parents, but rather represents a series of compromises that only partially pleased either Craig or his parents. Each side had to give a little in order to produce the contract.

As a general principle, it is probably a good idea to write down any agreements among adults and adolescents that concern time, work, or money.

4. behavior   5. smaller   6. back-up reinforcer

Key Ideas in Chapter 6

"Contracts" means writing down the specific behaviors and reinforcers agreed upon.

Negotiate all contracts, but the older the child, the more extensive negotiation should be.

7

What Kind of Reinforcers?

Probably the most available, useful, and important consequences are those such as praise, touch, attention, and smiles.
These are simple things. They occur hundreds of times each
day, and for each of us they are provided by a large number
of people.

If any one of these social reinforcers consistently
follows a child's behavior, then that behavior is likely to
occur again in the future. Most new behaviors are probably
learned by the child first observing others and then trying it
out himself (Bandura and Walters, 1963; Skinner, 1953). If
he receives social reinforcers for his performance, then he is
likely to try it again. If you remember to reinforce this new
behavior each time it occurs for several days or weeks, then
the behavior should become quite reliable. However, behavior
changes so slowly that many parents tend to give up trying to
produce changes this way. There is also another problem; a
review of research studies suggests that some problem children are less responsive to social reinforcers given by adults
(Patterson, Ray, and Shaw, 1968; Wahler, 1967). Parents of
such children who use *only* social reinforcers when they
implement a program of behavior change may have to work
that much harder to produce positive results.

Nonsocial Reinforcers

For these reasons, it is sometimes necessary to consider other ways to initially increase the effectiveness of parental management, such as using nonsocial reinforcers. Used together with social reinforcers, they usually bring about very rapid changes in behavior.

Many nonsocial reinforcers are taken for granted—the morning coffee break, the daily dessert after dinner, watching TV, and playing golf. For a child, nonsocial reinforcers include riding his bike, playing outside in the yard with friends, reading comics, or having no chores to do. These everyday things can be powerful reinforcers.

Homme (1970) showed that the key to the proper use of nonsocial reinforcers lies in the skill with which one arranges the "contingency contract." *First,* specify the behavior to be strengthened—"a little bit of studying"—*and then* provide the nonsocial reinforcer—"watching TV." This "first-and-then" principle has been shown by researchers such as Homme to have many practical possibilities for parents and teachers. *First* your child hangs up his coat, *and then* he gets his after-school snack. 1_____ he washes his face, *and then* he eats supper. *First* he eats his peas and corn, *and* 2 _____ he gets his dessert.

The first-and-then notion uses readily available natural consequences; it requires only a little imagination to identify consequences appropriate for you and for your child. They all have certain things in common. They occur often, at least once a day, and we tend to take them for granted. In contingency management we simply make it necessary to earn the good things in life. For example, you might earn the right to sit down at the dinner table by first requiring that you weigh yourself.

Take a "weak" behavior, one that seldom occurs, and require that it be performed before you have access to one of these nonsocial reinforcers that you take for granted. Con-

1. First   2. then

tingency management requires only that you identify natural consequences which occur regularly and specify the manner in which they are to be earned.

Contracting for Nonsocial Reinforcers

Contracts facilitate the use of nonsocial reinforcers in child management programs. Points are recorded each day so the child can observe his own progress. When he gets a specified number of points he earns some natural consequence which he values very much. For example, twenty points might earn a trip to the bowling alley with father, a Saturday afternoon movie, a model airplane, or a streamer for his bike. The points and the back-up reinforcer are negotiated with the child beforehand so that he understands exactly what the "game" is.

"Jane, you do lots of nice things around here but your room is still pretty messy. Nagging you every day about it doesn't work; besides, neither you nor I like that very much anyway. I have an idea about how to teach you to keep your room clean. I think it will be fun for you and also I won't have to nag you about it anymore.

"The way this game works is that you get a chance to earn something that you really want at the same time that you are learning to keep your room neat and picked up. Interested? OK. Here is the way it works. Each morning I check to see if you have made your bed and put away your clothes and toys. If all three things have been done, you get a point for that day; I mark it right here on this card.

"We will tape the card to the refrigerator so you can see it each day. What would you like to earn with your ten points? . . .No, a new bike is too expensive; pick something else. How about having Sally come and stay overnight for a pajama party? . . .OK, that is what we will do this week, and you might think of what you want to earn for next week."

Name _Jane_

Behavior: _Make bed and put away clothes and toys_

	M	T	W	T	F	S	S
1st week							
2nd week							
3rd week							
4th week							

Consequences: _Room neat in morning — 1 pt. Room neat in evening — 1 pt. 10 points means Sally can come over for a pajama party._

Every point the mother records acts as a nonsocial 3_____ for the child's keeping her room picked up. Naturally, the mother will also use 4_____ reinforcers to further strengthen the behavior.

Do not require that the room be perfect on the first day. If the bed was sloppily made, but an obvious attempt

3. reinforcer   4. social

70

was made, give her the point. You might suggest that if she can make it perfectly she will get two points. Model it for her and show her what you mean. Then, tear the bed up and have her try to reproduce what it is that you want. In this way you are being specific. She can literally see what it is that you want. Give her two points if she gets it correct during practice. *Don't be stingy with points or with social reinforcers.*

Do not debate with the child. Explain that you found some socks on the floor, so she received no point for that morning. Do not accept excuses. No Supreme Court defense on your part is required. Your arguing will reinforce her for initiating arguments in the future. If you forgot to put a mark down, or if she should have had two marks and you gave only one, apologize for it.

Whether you are using a contingency contract for the child to immediately earn a natural consequence or a point system which specifies a consequence to be earned several days hence, it is wise to write down the arrangement.

There are several kinds of contracts that are guaranteed *not* to work. If points are taken away for things the child did before the contract was set up, the child is likely to feel that it is unjust. The contract applies only to things which will happen from that point on. We have also tried several times to start each day with, say, ten points. Each time the child misbehaved, he lost a point. In retrospect, it should have been obvious that such a contract would make the child feel as if he could only lose. In any event, it did not work. The child must be able to gain points as well as lose them. *Be fair, but, above all, be reinforcing.*

The child should be encouraged to select his own back-up 5_____ . Also remember to select an initial level of performance that is appropriate for the child to insure his earning reinforcement during the very first stages. Do not scold or criticize; simply 6_____ those behaviors which are appropriate. Keep the steps 7_____ and specific. As the behavior comes under control you might

5. reinforcer   6. reinforce   7. small

71

increase the amount of work or the standards of performance, but discuss these increases with the child, always within
the context of how well he is doing at the present time.

Key Ideas in Chapter 7

The first-and-then principle makes use of natural consequences that occur every day.
Use contracts to facilitate the use of nonsocial reinforcers.
Don't be stingy with reinforcers; be fair, but, above all, be
reinforcing.

8

Time Out

Time Out Weakens Behavior

The term *"Time Out" (TO) means time out from reinforcement.* The young child is moved from a situation that is reinforcing problem behavior to one that is not at all reinforcing. This arrangement has proven to be a most effective means of producing *rapid* decreases in the occurrence of problem behaviors. It is also something that can replace spanking, which is the kind of punishment most parents use.

If you ignore undesirable behavior, it will be weakened. Given enough time, such an arrangement is very likely to work, but, in the meantime, the long-suffering parent or teacher has to put up with several hundred temper tantrums, teases, hits, or whines. TO is an extension of the idea of nonreinforcement, but extended in a way which makes it much more effective in bringing about rapid changes in behavior.

The child is removed from the situation where he receives many reinforcers and he is placed in a new situation where he receives few, if any. For example, if he teases, he might be placed in the bathroom for five minutes; this is a dull, nonreinforcing place. He is placed there every time he teases. The effect of a number of pairings of teasing and TO will be that the behavior is 1_____. Generally the effect is noticeable within three to four days.

Most parents have been trained by children to rely upon the two crutches of scolding and spanking. These parent behaviors will usually turn off the aversive behavior for a short time; and this short-term reduction in "pain" will act to 2_____ the parents for scolding and spanking. Unfortunately, *spanking and other physical punishment often produce an emotional aftermath that is unpleasant for both parent and child.* As most parents are reluctant to get involved in such an emotional scene very often, they spank only every tenth or hundredth time the problem behavior occurs. When they spank often depends upon how they happen to feel at the moment. What this means, of course, is that between spankings the child receives all kinds of reinforcement from his siblings. While he may periodically be spanked, adding up the amount of strengthening and weakening involved would show that the behavior is reduced only on a short-term basis and actually shows long-term increases in rate.

Parents who are willing to track very carefully and punish each time are effective but then they must pay the emotional price tag attached to this approach. There may be an emotional price tag attached to the first few times TO is used. *TO is a mild punishment but it is an effective substitute for hitting, spanking, yelling, and lecturing.* It can be used a dozen times a day at little cost to the parent. Rather than waiting until the child's behavior is so obnoxious that you are upset and angry, TO can be introduced early in the behavioral chain. It is used when the children are just beginning to get wound up and before the teasing and fighting begin.

First Steps in Using TO

In using TO you would *begin by pinpointing and counting both the problem behavior and the pro-social behavior that*

1. weakened   2. reinforce

will take its place. It is generally a good idea to first begin the reinforcement point program involved in strengthening the pro-social behavior so that the overall amount of reinforcement for the child is increased; make it indirectly reinforcing for the child to participate in the program. In other words, before applying nonreinforcement and TO you must be sure the child is receiving adequate 3_____ for some behaviors. If you tend to use very few social reinforcers in interacting with your child, *make doubly sure that you have a reinforcement program underway before using nonreinforcement or TO.* Reinforcement and shaping procedures should be the solid foundations upon which you build child management procedures, with the main emphasis upon positive reinforcement, shaping pro-social behaviors, and using contracts and point programs.

TO is most effective for high rate behaviors found in younger children between the ages of two and twelve. For older children, it might be necessary to negotiate some other type of aversive consequences for certain behaviors. For example, coming in late in the evening would not earn TO but would mean "grounded for a week." Swearing would lead to neither TO nor a lecture, but rather to the calm statement "That word cost you 25¢." These consequences must be established in advance and preferably written down.

A Place for TO

The first consideration in using TO lies in the selection of a place. It should have several characteristics, but primarily it should be *very dull.* It should symbolize all that is nonreinforcing. That means no toys, no TV, no books, *no people.* In the home, the bathroom is the most likely spot. For the child who is extremely active or destructive, it might be necessary to remove all of the objects from the medicine cabinet. If, as frequently happens, the child runs water all

3. reinforcement

over the floor, he earns a natural consequence of cleaning it up (after his TO is completed). Give no lectures; simply state, "You must clean up the bathroom floor before you watch TV tonight." Clearly state what the 4_____ will be for noncompliance to the request. Be specific about what you mean by "clean up the mess," and spell out the consequence for not "cleaning up the mess."

For the classroom a screen in one corner of the room with a chair placed behind it is adequate for TO for most unmanageable children. Make sure that the child is not readily visible to the other children. Extremely unmanageable children may have to serve TO in the nurse's office for a day or two before the screen-chair ensemble is effective.

Parents often have strong feelings about putting their child into the bathroom and make a case for putting a chair in the hallway or in the corner as alternatives. However, this usually does not work, because there are people in these areas and people are just naturally reinforcing. One of the first requirements for proper use of TO is that it must be in a 5_____ place. If you observe the amount of social interaction that occurs around a child sitting in a corner of the kitchen, you can easily ascertain that it is not non-reinforcing. In fact, he may get more reinforcement there than at most other times in his day. But collect data and see. If your data show that standing in the corner for five minutes is decelerating the behavior you want to change, then it "works" for your child. Three days of consistent use of TO should reduce the rates of most problem behaviors.

Using TO Effectively

Many parents say, "But I've used TO for years and it didn't work. I send him to his room all the time and it never works." Closer checking reveals that the parent did *not* send him to the bedroom every time, and that the room had a full

4. consequence   5. dull

complement of toys, comic books, and TV. By definition, this is *not* TO. *TO must be used consistently and carried out in a place that is essentially* 6 _____.

TO differs in several respects from the normal expedient of sending the child to his room. Most parents do *not* send the child to his room every time. Most children's bedrooms are full of reinforcing things. *TO is used for only a short period of time (three to five minutes),* while "being sent to your room" could mean a sentence ranging from thirty minutes to all day. These long sentences are for the parents' benefit; they feel better with the child out of the way. TO, on the other hand, keeps the child out of the parents' way for only three to five minutes and the parents must work hard to keep track of the time so the child does not spend long periods of time in isolation. Research with children has shown that one to five minutes of TO is as effective as twenty to thirty minutes of TO (Patterson and White, 1969). Set a kitchen timer when the child goes into TO so that the end of the time interval is clearly signaled for both parent and child.

Putting a child into TO requires some skill. The arrangement should be specified beforehand so that you do not find yourself attempting to explain TO when both you and the child are very angry.

"I know you have trouble remembering not to interrupt people when they are talking. I also know that you are tired of having your mother and me nag you about it all of the time. We have a program that will help you practice not interrupting people. I think it might even be fun for you.

"First, if you can go all evening without interrupting anyone, you get five points. Each time you interrupt, you lose one point. We will keep track each day. When you get twenty points, that is worth three comic books; or is there something else you would like to earn?

6. dull, nonreinforcing

"To help with the practice we are also going to use TO. Each time you interrupt someone, we will tell you and then you go into TO. We will set the timer so that it rings at the end of five minutes. You go into the bathroom and wait for it to go off; then you come out."

Some parents arrange for any family member who interrupts to go into Time Out. This seems a fair arrangement. When the actual occasion for TO arrives, be calm. Do not scold or nag. "Whoops, you did it. That was an interruption. Five minutes in TO; I will set the timer so that you know when to come out."

Do not debate the legality of the situation; be very firm. If he insists on debating, inform him that each minute of debate means another minute in 7_____ . Ignore his arguments other than to inform him "one minute more," "two minutes more," and so forth. When he has earned thirty to forty minutes of time, you might inform him that if he does not go into TO within the next minute, he will lose TV rights for that night (or lose dessert, the bicycle, or the right to leave the yard). Be certain that this back-up consequence is followed through on that very night. If you forget to back up your statements, then you have really lost the interchange and things will be worse the next time. Do not physically drag him into TO; calmly state what the consequence for his non-compliance is and then walk away.

Some children, really well trained in manipulating adults, may say something like, "Go ahead, put me in the bathroom; I like it in there." Many children can actually talk their parents out of using TO. Go ahead and use TO, collect data on the behavior you are decelerating, and see what three days of *consistent* application of TO does. His words may or may not tell you what will work. Your data tell you what works.

Many children will attempt to come out of the TO room, talk to people, yell, cry, or kick the door. If they

7. Time Out

break anything in the room during TO, then naturally they must pay for it out of their allowance. For each kick, yell, or attempt to peek out of the TO room, add one more minute of TO. Tell him when he gets out that each response costs him more time. Each minute of yelling or crying would elicit the same response. If he comes out before time is up and refuses to re-enter, state your back-up consequence and then ignore him. "Unless you go to TO immediately, your bike will be locked up; it will stay locked up for two days." Do not become engaged in arguments, debates, or lectures about whether you have the right to do this.

If the child was originally sent into TO for failure to comply with some request, repeat the request when he comes out of TO. If he noncomplies again, return him to 8_____. When he has completed that round, repeat the 9_____ .

If the children act up in the car or at the store, they can be told that they are earning TO, assuming that the procedure has previously been in effect in the home. The child is placed in TO as soon as you arrive home.

Using TO In a Behavior Change Program

Kurt was a nine-year-old boy living in a comfortable home. He kept the family continually off-balance with high rates of teasing his younger sister, humiliating his mother, and non-complying to requests made by either parent. The parents often engaged in bitter arguments about whose fault it was. They tried all of the usual tactics, trying to correct his behavior and their own. Spankings and severe punishments had no effect, nor did bribes. He was placed on a point system in which he earned points for each hour during which one of the behaviors did not occur; and he earned TO for each occurrence of the behavior. The graph on page 80 shows what happened to "noncompliance," "humiliation," and "teasing."

8. Time Out   9. request

During the baseline observation period Kurt was inflicting three or four of these behaviors on members of his family every hour. By the end of the first day of the program he was displaying only one of these behaviors every two or three hours. Results are not usually this dramatic. For many families, the first day may actually show an increase in the rate of problem behaviors.

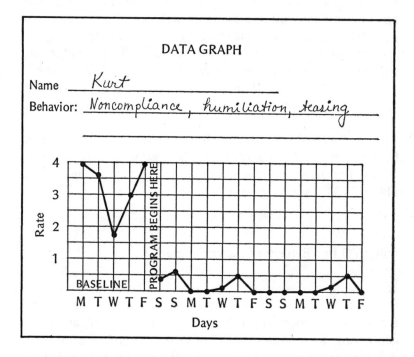

DATA GRAPH

Name ___Kurt___

Behavior: ___Noncompliance, humiliation, teasing___

Notice that even though Kurt had been on the program for several days, there was one point where the rate of problem behavior again climbed to .2 and then .65 per hour. This happened on the third 10_____ and 11_____.
On these "bad days" the parents simply used TO and again brought the problems under control. At the end of two

10. Wednesday   11. Thursday

weeks this was a much different home, a much happier one for everyone concerned, including Kurt. Even when the behavior is reasonably under control, use TO whenever the problems recur in the future. Behavior does not just disappear; rather, it will tend to recur from time to time. When this happens, your reactions will determine whether the problem behaviors are strengthened or weakened. You do construct your own social world, but it is also up to you to keep it in repair.

When using TO be certain that you remain calm. In addition, be sure to apply it each 12_____ the problem behavior occurs. *Both parents participate in using the point program and TO.* It is often the case that the father is particularly reluctant to use either one.

Often, there are regular chains of events which lead up to the problem behavior. TO should be used to interrupt these chains. For example, hitting is usually the outcome of a prolonged argument or a teasing interchange. If this is the case, use TO to weaken the earlier arguing or teasing.

There is one form of punishment that seems to be similar to Time Out, but in our experience has not worked so well. Several families have tried "grounding" as a punishment. When the child earned many minus points, he was grounded in his bedroom for the remainder of the day. Some parents have used several days' grounding as a consequence for severe problems such as stealing or truancy. It is our experience that this simply doesn't work very well. Perhaps there remain available too many reinforcers for the child to sample while being grounded. While grounding seems to be preferred by many as a punishment, we have found several hours of work, raking, painting, pulling weeds, or scrubbing, to be far more effective.

It has probably occurred to you that there are really many variations on the TO theme. For example, some parents have simply removed themselves from the home for a

12. time

half-hour or longer when the children's behavior gets too obnoxious. Married couples also report the use of "stony silence" which may last for hours or days as a kind of prolonged TO. In all of these instances, the individual is deciding that he will no longer provide reinforcement for the person whose behavior he is attempting to alter. TO, then, is a natural consequence already in use by many persons.

Key Ideas in Chapter 8

TO means time out from reinforcement.
Physical punishment often has an emotional aftermath.
TO is a mild, but effective, punishment.
Before using TO,
>pinpoint and count the problem behavior;
>reinforce pro-social behavior more often; and
>explain the program to the child.
To use TO effectively,
>parents must be consistent;
>a very dull place must be used for TO;
>TO should last only 1-5 minutes; and
>both parents should participate.

Section III

APPLICATIONS TO ORDINARY MANAGEMENT PROBLEMS

This section details the application of the procedures for handling problems that come up in almost all families. Each of us does things that upset the people with whom we live. How do we manage to keep these "little things" from accumulating? We probably handle most of them by the simple expedient of discussing them and then one or both persons change their behavior. These changes are reinforced by the other person and there is one more almost imperceptible change in the family system.

However, simply discussing and labeling problems does not always work. There are times when a spouse or an adolescent simply will not change his behavior even though it is terribly disrupting to the rest of the family. One should not *impose* a point system or Time Out to remediate problems, even with a six-year-old, and the process of negotiating programs becomes increasingly complex as we work with an adolescent child or spouse. Chapter 9 describes a process for learning negotiation and exchange skills. The work was based in part upon two years of systematic work with distressed married couples (Patterson and Cobb, 1971a; Patterson and Hops, 1972) and upon our more recent clinical experiences.

After interviewing and surveying a large number of mothers of preschool children, it became clear that most of them had several areas of concern in raising their children. For these families, there were a dozen or more difficulties that showed up again and again. They were perhaps not of such a magnitude as to require professional assistance, but they were sufficiently troublesome to be a point of real concern. Because of our interest in developing "prevention" procedures, we became interested in these complaints. Since 1973, we have pilot-tested seven programs for dealing with things most frequently noted as areas of concern by the survey sample. These programs are covered in Chapter 10. As more of these programs are innovated and field-tested, they will be included in later revisions of *Families.*

9

Adult Behavior Change Techniques: Negotiation and Exchange

Thus far we have concentrated upon the skills required for the adult learning to deal with younger children. While they are important, these skills will probably not handle problems that come up among older members of the family. Reinforcement of desirable behavior and nonreinforcement for undesirable behavior *might* produce slow changes over long periods of time. However, each of the adults in the family is being reinforced for many things by people who are not in the immediate family. Parents and adolescent children are influenced by their co-workers and friends; the older the individual and the more diverse his outside contacts, the more difficult it is to change his behavior. The reason for the difficulty lies in the fact that with increasing age, it becomes close to impossible to retrain all of the people who 1_____ him for his usual way of doing things.

   It is necessary, therefore, to follow somewhat different procedures in programming changes for older members of the family. While we will continue using social reinforcers, pinpointing problem behaviors, and keeping data, it will be necessary to explore some additional means of negotiating changes in each other's behavior. These procedures are

1. reinforce

analogous to "bartering" and to modern sociological exchange theory (Homans, 1961; Lederer and Jackson, 1968).

NEGOTIATION

The Need for Negotiation

In order to live together in a closed group, it is necessary to negotiate for behavior change. If individuals get into conflict at work, there are rules and procedures for arbitrating such changes. If these procedures don't work, you can generally avoid these unpleasant people. If all else fails, you may decide to leave. The rules, arbitration procedures, and relative freedom to avoid or leave usually keep conflict within manageable limits. In the home, however, these safety valves are not operating. There are seldom clear-cut rules for arbitration and it is almost impossible to leave.

To make the problem more difficult, people within the family are constantly changing over time. This is particularly true of the adolescent who is being trained by his peers. Each change requires other family members to adjust by somehow changing too. For example, when the adolescent learns to drive the family car, this will have an effect on other family members.

Requests for behavior change are a normal part of living together as a family. Interestingly enough, they usually are concerned with "little things." How does a wife go about getting her husband to pick up his clothes that he leaves lying about every day? This is a small thing. On the other hand, he does it every day. If one after another of these small things pile up and do not change, their accumulative effect is to produce large-scale conflicts. Each small problem is added to the growing pile of unresolved problems. In many instances, the victim spends a good deal of time brooding about the various grievances, but feels powerless to change the situation. Over an extended period of time, this accumulation of "little things" can change the way we feel about each other.

Finally, one day the accumulation bursts like an avalanche upon the relationship and the other person may be presented with an astonishing collection of ancient grievances.

Setting Up a Negotiation Session

It is important to discuss problems as they arise. The longer you wait the more likely this brooding process will begin. In our clinical experience, brooding is often followed by a rising tide of anger and resentment. These feelings make conse-quent behavior change doubly difficult.

As soon as the problem arises, *arrange a time and place for a discussion.* Clearly label what it is that you wish to do.

"Tim, a problem has come up that I must talk to you about. Could we take fifteen minutes after dinner tonight? I'd like to tell you what I think the difficulty is and see if we can solve it."

Select a time when both of you are relatively relaxed, e.g., *not* before dinner when people are generally tired and hungry, and *certainly* not late in the evening when you are both in bed preparing for sleep. *Never* discuss problems on the way to a party.

For some couples, the accumulation of conflicts has gone on for years. Both persons desperately wish for relief of some kind, so each moment alone together is seized by one person as being an appropriate time for "discussing" one or more conflicts. These "discussions" invariably degenerate to arguments and fights. Select a time and a quiet place for negotiation where you will be relatively free from interrup-tions. Negotiation sessions should be arranged in advance. Do not surprise the other person; he is supposed to be your ally in the negotiation process.

Rules for the Session

Participants in the session should have read this material, so that everyone will be playing by the same rules. A cardinal rule for the sessions is that *the victim is always right*. Other investigators have noted the importance of this rule (Lederer and Jackson, 1968). The victim is saying that he has been hurt by something which the other person has done. There is no argument about whether or not he is hurting. If the victim says he has been hurt, then it is a fact.

During the five or ten minutes in which the victim describes the situation, the only thing required of the other person is that he listen. It is not necessary to explain, deny, or apologize. It is only necessary to sit quietly and 2_____ . There will be a very important contribution made by this person at a later time in the session.

The victim has center stage for 3_____ ___ _____ minutes. He also has an extremely important rule to follow. *The victim describes only two things: what the other person did, and how it made the victim feel.* The victim does not try to guess why the other person did these things. The victim does not say the other member is a bad person. There is no punishment or criticism. Describe the problem and describe how it made you 4_____ . Do 5_____ attack the other person. If you do attack, you may get temporary revenge but it is almost certain that the negotiation will fail.

"If you leave here and go looking for work in California, I'm afraid we won't have enough money to pay the rent during the first month. I'm also afraid I can't handle the kids all by myself . . . I think I will be very lonely."

In this situation, these simple facts tell the husband what problems must be resolved. Now there is a possibility of

2. listen   3. five to ten   4. feel   5. not

90

working them out. On the other hand, if she had presented it as follows, there would be very little chance of negotiating.

"You just can't keep a job. Every time it goes well for a couple of months, you decide to leave and find another one. How do I know I can trust you? If you go to California and find a job, you will just spend the money. You don't love me anymore; you are just looking for an excuse to leave me with the kids."

In this example, the victim made two errors: She played the game of guessing her husband's intentions/motives, and she in effect said that he was a bad person. This statement of the problem can only lead to his defending himself and attacking her in turn. If the victim attacks the other person, then he can expect to be immediately 6_____ in turn. If, as victim, it is difficult to restrain yourself, then practice by first writing down what it is you will say.

In any given session, the victim should cover only one problem; it is an enormous temptation to run through the entire range of grievances. Do not give in to that temptation; if you do, effective behavior change is unlikely. The victim should keep the description brief; even five minutes is pushing the limit somewhat.

When the victim has completed the description, then *the other person is to paraphrase* what the victim said. It is an amazing fact that many spouses have trained themselves not to "hear" the other spouse even if the communications are shouted. Many parent-adolescent interchanges have this same quality. After so much punishment, people stop hearing each other. The paraphrase should be just a sentence or two: "If I go to California, you're afraid you won't get enough money and you'll be lonely."

Notice that he did not criticize his wife, nor did he try to explain why he wanted to go to California. If there have

6. attacked

been heated interchanges about their problems in the past, then it is the other person's turn to play the role of "victim."

"I can't find the kind of work in this area that I've been trained to do. If you insist on living here, I'll end up making a lot less money. I'm going to feel cheated—like I haven't had a chance to see what I can really do."

He stated what it was that his wife did that caused the problem, i.e., she insisted that he remain where they were. He did not guess at her motivation nor did he say she was a bad person:

"You are just like your mother. That's why you want to stay here—just so the two of you can run my life. When are you going to grow up? You have to leave momma someday."

Following his description, then it was the wife's turn to paraphrase what it was that she had done that caused him to be hurt: "If I make you stay here, you're going to feel put down in your work—like you haven't had a fair chance."

Such an interchange does not necessarily lead to an immediate solution. It is probably wise to end the session after the paraphrasing work is completed. Give people a chance to think about these facts. Chances are both persons have a somewhat different perspective on the problem. They need a chance now to think it over and see if there are some compromises which might be made. In the example used here, the husband might arrange for a job and sign over part of his check to his wife before leaving; or arranging for a loan might make it possible for her to accompany him to look for a new job.

If no compromise is forthcoming, then they might arrange for a second session in which they discuss a contract. This stage of negotiation is described in the next section.

EXCHANGE

Conflict

Conflict arises when one person demands immediate change in the behavior of another person and the other person non-complies. These demands are often accompanied by aversive statements. *One person demands immediate change; the other refuses: This defines* 7_____ . For example, the statement "Shut up, you idiot" is a demand for immediate behavior 8_____ . It also contains the negative evaluation term "idiot" which is 9 _____ to the other person. The use of aversive words makes it likely that the other person will counterattack rather than comply. In this situation, behavior will not change.

By this definition it takes 10_____ people to have a conflict—one who demands immediate changes in behavior and one who refuses to comply. If the interchange has occurred many times in the past, and no changes in behavior followed, then the exchanges are more likely to be accompanied by aversive statements by both persons.

"Please pick up your clothes. Every day I have to go around and pick up after you. I'm not your mother. You act just like a little boy." He hardly looks up from reading the paper. "Listen, I work eight hours a day, five days a week. When I come home I want peace and quiet, and I sure as hell don't want to be nagged. You are just like your mother—everything has to be perfect. Nag, nag, all of the time!" At this point her voice raises and she shouts, "I'm not a slave in this house, either. . . ."

She is demanding behavior change and punishing at the same time. When she does this, the spouse is likely to respond

7. conflict   8. change   9. aversive   10. two

in kind. What you have in this situation is two people 11_____ each other, but no behavior changes. After hundreds of these interchanges, two people are likely to stop listening to each other and may even stop interacting with each other. *Punishing another person by insulting him, yelling at him, or nagging him about past wrongs will only lead to a situation where the other person either avoids you or attacks you in turn.* In any case, *both of you will be sidetracked.*

You may try a hundred times, but each time the dialogue gets sidetracked. Instead of designing a behavior change program, you end up hurting each other. When two people are discussing a program for behavior change, the use of 12_____ will lead to 13_____. After months of unsuccessful effort so many different problems have accumulated that no time or place in the household is free from strife.

Negotiation

Arrange for a discussion time and place. Select a quiet room and select only the two or three persons directly involved. Agree upon a negotiating time: Literally make an appointment. At first, the sessions should be relatively brief, for example, ten to twenty minutes. It is probably best to keep half an hour as the upper limit. Work on only one problem per session. If a particular problem is pressing, it might be wise to provide for regular daily sessions. In advanced stages of conflict, the mere presence of the person in the room becomes a stimulus for hassling; going in the car together to a party can set the occasion for bitter strife. If this is the case for you, do not negotiate at other times during the day. If a problem comes up, say, "Well, OK. That sounds important, but let's wait until our discussion time at 4:00 today." If both members do this, they will teach each other to stop the continuous, mutual harassment.

11. punishing   12. punishment   13. sidetracking

After you have selected a regular 14_____ and 15_____ for your negotiations, there are rules of procedure to follow. Each person should come to the discussion armed only with paper and pencil. Everyone observes and labels aversive comments; these include attempts to go over past wrongs and grievances, insulting statements, attempts to blame the other person for the present difficulties, and threats. If you are well-practiced combatants, you will be amazed at how much of your interaction is characterized by these behaviors. When one occurs, the offended member must label it: "That was a zap (punishment)." It is recorded in the logbook. Agree in advance how many such occurrences are tolerable, e.g., two, three, four. When this number occurs, the meeting is terminated for that day. You may find that many of your first meetings are interrupted early. You might decide to use monetary fines so that each zap costs the person a quarter. The victim is always the one to decide if he has just been punished. He knows when he has been hurt. Don't let the punisher talk you out of it. "Oh, was that a zap? No one would call *that* a zap!" If the victim says it hurts, it *is* a zap.

The successful design of behavior change programs presupposes that you first teach each other to stop punishing when discussing behavior change. You must be able to discuss conflicts with "zero zapping."

Exchange

When negotiating, take turns so that each person has equal time. Do not use your time in going over ancient histories of hurts and wrongs. Stay in the present and *pinpoint changes in the behavior of the other person that would make your life more pleasant.* Talk only about the 16_____ and be 17_____ . List the specific behaviors of the other person that you would like to have changed. Take five or ten minutes to pinpoint one problem behavior. During that time

14. time   15. place   16. present   17. specific

the other person just listens: no arguments or debates while the speaker specifies what the behaviors are that hurt him. During the pinpointing, the speaker must also specify one positive behavior displayed by the other person that makes him feel good. Stay in the 18_____, be specific, and pinpoint both a positive and an aversive behavior in each session. Only 19_____ problem should be discussed each session.

Pinpointing simply means that you be 20_____ . List which behaviors of the other person please you and which you wish to have 21_____. For example, "I wish my wife were a better housekeeper" is not pinpointing a behavior. A pinpoint must be so clear that the behavior can be observed and counted. The listener might help at this point by asking, "What does 'better housekeeper' mean?"

"Well, you know, I'd like to have the living room picked up when I come home." His wife sits writing down the statement, looking a bit angry, but says nothing. "I'd like to have you put your stuff away that you leave in the bathroom." At this point she slams the notebook down on the floor and retorts, "Some of that is your junk, too, and the kids', so what about that?" "OK, Zelda, that was a zap. You attacked me and didn't let me finish. Save it for your turn. I'd like to have the dishes washed and put away, too. OK? I like the way you bring me coffee at night when I'm reading."

The behaviors which he listed were specific and there was little argument about whether or not the behavior had occurred. The wife made a similar list of specific messy behaviors displayed by her husband, including throwing clothes on the closet floor, leaving newspapers strewn around the floor, and storing junk in the garage. It may require several discussion sessions to pinpoint. You have plenty of time; keep your

18. present   19. one   20. specific   21. changed

negotiations short and calm. If you don't solve a problem, come back to it later.

Once the lists are written down, you are ready for the next step: *Exchange pinpointed items.* Beginning with item one on her husband's list, Zelda agreed that she would not leave her articles lying about the living room. However, he in turn must pick up the newspapers he throws on the floor each evening. She also agreed that the dishes would be washed and stored away if he would neatly box and store his "collection" in the garage. When the list of specific behaviors is available, it is surprising how well the exchange can be negotiated.

Record all lists and exchanges. Items and agreements are easily forgotten by even the best-intentioned people. Protect yourselves from future disagreements—"I said. . . ." "No, you really said. . . ."—by the simple expedient of writing them down. These contracts are too important to leave to fallible memory.

Before you can trade behaviors to be changed, the problem behaviors must, as a first step, be 22_____ . Then 23_____ them down. Good intentions and writing things down don't necessarily produce behavior change. Most persons experience a brief honeymoon period after making a contract. However, as so often happens after making New Year's resolutions, they slip back into old ways and the problem behaviors may reappear. For this reason, *the last step in exchange may be crucial, for it makes provisions for consequences.* These consequences reduce the likelihood of slipping back into old ways. Each person should stipulate what the consequence will be for his own violating of the agreement. Zelda and her husband agreed that any articles of clothing left lying about would be deposited in a "Saturday Box." This contribution by Lindsley requires that deposits remain in the box until Saturday, at which time they are returned to their owners. Fines might also be levied; the amounts should be agreed upon in advance and written into the contract.

22. specific   23. write

Each of us is continually changing. It is likely that two or more people who live together will have a continuing need to negotiate the changes in each other's behaviors. A change in one family member may pose problems for the other members, and negotiation and renegotiation may be necessary. Once a contract has been set up, it is often necessary to renegotiate part or all of the contract. In this context it might be interesting to contemplate agreements with spouses to accelerate behaviors which both agree would be desirable. One spouse might, for example, trade an hour of reading for his spouse's taking a relaxing walk. Why not negotiate "growth" or "self-improving" behaviors?

An Exchange Program

Bill and Betty were young, attractive people. They were socially skilled and both moderately successful in their fields. She managed a small boutique and he ran a small business from an office in their home. Their two children were both in school, but in the past year had been showing increasing rates of out-of-control behavior at home and in school. While the parents were able to learn how to handle the children's problems by participating in a parent training program, they returned some months later to describe a marriage which had been steadily deteriorating for the past few years.

They found that most of their time spent together was a setting for endless bickering and increasingly intense conflicts. Within the past month the husband had mentioned the possibility of divorce. Many of their conflicts centered around "her working" and "her coldness" and "his nagging" and "his worrying about money." They received a series of half a dozen training sessions in which they were trained to pinpoint problems without sidetracking, negotiate exchanges and consequences, and write contracts. The details of these procedures and the data showing the changes in behaviors are presented in reports published elsewhere (Patterson and Cobb, 1971a; Patterson and Hops, 1972).

They wrote a series of contracts which laid the groundwork for profound changes in both their own behavior and the behavior of their children. Writing the first contract required several weeks of effort. It was particularly difficult for the husband to pinpoint what it was about his wife's behavior that bothered him and what it was that was pleasing to him. For example, he began by saying that "she is nice to be around." After some searching, it turned out that he really liked it when she would sit and talk to him about his work and the family. Her sitting and talking about her own work, or sitting and fixing her nails was not a particularly pleasing behavior. She, on the other hand, could be quite specific in saying that she appreciated his getting supper ready when she came in late from work.

The following contract was their first effort and was constructed under close supervision.

AGREEMENT NO. 1

Changes that Betty wants to see in Bill:

1. Discuss money only once a week for 15 minutes or less.

2. Nag only once a month.

3. No nagging about her job unless the routine is changed.

4. If he slips up and does more nagging than this, the consequence will be to buy her a dress on the household account ($20).

Changes that Bill wants to see in Betty:

1. Deviations from the present work routine are upsetting. The present routine includes: Monday, 9-5:30; Tuesday, 5-9; off Wednesday; Thursday, 5-9; Friday, 9-1; off Saturday and Sunday. If the routine is broken (Betty comes home late or works on a weekend), this costs Betty $5 from her checking account.

2. When Bill can afford to give Betty $100 per month for herself, then she quits work.

Betty	_B. ll_
Betty	Bill

For a few days things were wonderful. Bill did not nag and Betty managed to stay with her work schedule. However, in the next week there was sufficient backsliding to cost both of them a substantial amount of money. When the first "nag" occurred, Betty felt that the whole thing was rather hopeless and that Bill could not change. She also said that the $20 just was not that important to her and maybe she should just let it go by. However, she was encouraged to collect her reward and to believe that over time Bill would change.

Both Bill and Betty collected consequences for the next week and gradually the behaviors in their first contract were brought under control. At this point they were encouraged to try some further negotiations for other problems. After their experience with the first contract, they were able to pinpoint the problems much more clearly.

AGREEMENT NO. 2

Pinpoints for Bill:

1. Bill hangs his clothes on bedposts and throws them on the bureau. He shall pay $5 each time this happens.
2. Bill throws newspapers on the floor when he's finished reading. When he does this, he shall mop the floor and/or wash the windows for not less than 3 days.
3. Bill will not replace his shaving materials after using. If he leaves them out, Betty can hide them for not more than 3 days.

Pinpoints for Betty:

1. Betty does not place her shoes on her shoe rack after coming home from work. Betty shall pay the amount of $5 for each pair of shoes not placed on the shoe rack.
2. Betty leaves dinner dishes overnight. If this happens, Betty must wash the Volkswagen and clean the interior.
3. Betty does not keep her bathroom neat. Bill can put any articles left out into a hiding place for not more than 3 days.

___Betty_____   ___Bill_____
Betty   Bill

100

As the rate of conflicts dropped, Betty and Bill began discussing more general aspects of their marriage and family life. Each relationship has some implied agreements which must be specified and pinpointed. From their discussions they discovered the importance of each of them living a separate life as well as a life as a member of the family. Bill, for example, had given up all of his former interests and friends. Betty, on the other hand, had become so immersed in her work that she was not too involved as a member of the family. The following general agreements and exchanges were worked out entirely by Bill and Betty.

AGREEMENT NO. 3

Spending more time alone—Bill will play golf and Betty will get a baby sitter and do her thing alone (spend some time with her friends). This shall occur not more than once a week. If one party chooses not to do this, that is all right. But if the other party chooses to do his or her thing, he or she may. If Bill chooses to do something other than golf, he may do whatever he wishes. This shall be strictly during the daytime.

Spending more time together—take weekend trips not less than three times a year. Betty shall see that proper arrangements are made for the children. A time shall be set for this and if one party refuses to go at this time, the consequences will be that the dissenting party will have to sacrifice his or her time alone (as in paragraph I). It is all right if both parties agree not to go at the planned time.

Bill has permitted Betty to work more hours, provided she does not work more than two nights a week and no weekends, or perhaps one-half day on Saturdays. This has to follow a stable schedule during the week. The consequences are $5 for every time she works an irregular schedule. If Bill harasses Betty during a normal routine in schedule, then he owes her $5.

Betty	_Bill_
Betty	Bill

There were satisfying reductions in rates of conflicts within the home. They spent more time talking with each other and more time together as a family. At the time of this writing, there has been no divorce. Most importantly, both felt that they had produced changes in their own behavior and felt they could handle similar problems in the future.

It is necessary for adults to negotiate for changes in behavior:
> arrange a time and place for negotiating sessions; and discuss problems as they arise.

In the negotiating session,
> the victim is always right;
> the victim describes what the other person did, and how it made him feel; and
> the listener paraphrases.

Conflict is a demand for immediate change followed by a noncompliance.

Aversive statements lead to more aversive statements or to sidetracking.

Contract an exchange program:
> pinpoint pleasing behaviors;
> exchange pinpointed items;
> record all exchanges; and
> arrange consequences for violating the agreement.

10

Child Management Problems

SO YOUR CHILD TEASES?*

If your three- to six-year-old does any of the following about once an hour, you have a "teaser" on your hands: grabs things away from other children; pushes, hits, kicks, or throws things; calls names and makes faces; interrupts other children as they play; or has loud yelling matches about who "owns" something or whose turn it is. Most young children may be expected to do these kinds of things once or twice a day.

If you decide to teach your child to cut down on teasing, buy a box of gold stars, and tape the gold star chart to your refrigerator door. *Write down on the chart the specific things your child does* that are teases. Pick the things he does at least once a day or more as your "target." *Explain the program to your child.*

"There is a lot of yelling, fighting, crying, and teasing going on. I'm going to help you practice so it won't happen so often. See the chart here on the door? Each time a tease happens, I'm going to put a mark in the box. Each day has its

---

* The writer particularly wishes to thank Matt Fleischman for pilot-testing this program.

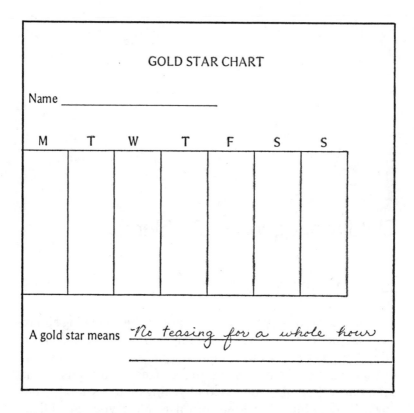

GOLD STAR CHART

Name _____

M	T	W	T	F	S	S

A gold star means _No teasing for a whole hour_

own box; see, here is for today. If you go a whole hour with no teases, then you get a gold star in the box. How many stars do you think you will get today?"

Do not nag or scold when he teases. Simply say, "That's a tease!" *Do not argue or debate* with him. Just put a check in the square for that day and that hour. Record it each time in as calm a voice as you can.

When he has been home for an hour with no teases, say, "Hey, it has really been nice. No teases for an hour! What a big boy you are! Should I put the gold star up or do you want to do it?" Give him the star even if he has been watching TV alone and not playing with anyone. Be as enthusiastic as you can!

For many teasers, the gold star approval game is all that is necessary. For them, the teasing decreases within two weeks and stays at an acceptable level. If you continue to let him know how much you appreciate his not teasing, it will stay there.

Some children, however, require a little more powerful program; they improve for a week or two but then slip back into their old ways in spite of the gold stars and the approval. For them, we advise the use of Time Out. You should read about how to do this before you try it (see Chapter 8).

TOILET TRAINING THREE-YEAR-OLDS

When the normal child is twenty-four months or older, he can learn to stay dry. But you have to teach him. Generally, you can teach him to do this in about two or three weeks.

Tape the gold star chart to the refrigerator door. Buy a pair of training pants and a box of gold stars and then explain the program to him.

"I'm going to help you practice staying dry. Every time you go to the bathroom, you get a gold star on your chart. You also get a snack. Why don't you go to the potty right now?"

If the child refuses to go to the bathroom, do not force him, do not nag or scold. If he does go, even a little bit, then say something like "That's good!" Be enthusiastic. "Now, we put a gold star on the chart, like so. What would you like for your snack today?"

At dinner in the evening, announce to the father how many times the child went to the toilet. On those days where he manages to stay dry, take a crayon and write a large D at the bottom of the column for that day, and make sure that this is also announced at the dinner table.

When the child forgets and wets his pants, have him immediately rinse the pants out in the sink and put them in the dryer. Have a sponge right there in the bathroom so that he can clean up any mess he makes on the floor by spilling water and soap. Do this every time he wets his pants.

Do not nag or scold: Be calm. "Oh, oh! You forgot and wet your pants. OK, let's go into the bathroom and I'll show you how to wash them."

Put some water in the basin, take soap and lightly soap the pants and scrub them, and then let him finish the task. When he spills water on the floor, show him how to mop it up with a sponge. Show him how to rinse the pants and then how to put them in the dryer. "OK, now you have to wait until the pants are dry because you only have one pair, so you'll sit here and wait. I'll see you in a little while. Bye-bye."

BEDWETTING: A SIMPLE FIRST APPROACH*

The problem of nighttime wetting for children four years and older is one that is encountered by many parents. Some parents seem to be able to train their child to stay dry with little or no difficulties. For others, the learning seems to be difficult. We believe that part of the difference in effectiveness lies in the kind of program used by parents. The program outlined here is a simple one, one that you might try first. If this program does not bring an end to the bedwetting, then other methods should be tried.

The child is told that wetting the bed at night is a problem. "Now that you are a big boy, it is time to learn to stop wetting the bed at night. I'll bet you would like to learn how to stop that, wouldn't you? Yes, and then we wouldn't have to wash the sheets every morning. I'm going to help you practice so you can stop wetting the bed. OK? What would you like to earn while you practice? You will be able to earn something each day."

Make a list of inexpensive readily available reinforcers he would enjoy, e.g., extra cereal snacks, gold stars, ten minutes of reading to him just before bedtime. The child should be told that if he remains dry during the night, he will

---

* The author wishes to thank Elizabeth Steinboch for her assistance in field-testing an earlier version of the program.

get the reinforcers the very next day. For the first week, reinforcers should be administered daily, every other day the second week, every fourth or fifth day the third week, and so on until the reinforcers are phased out. Post the gold star chart and place a gold star for each dry night. When the child stays dry for a night, announce it at the dinner table with a special hat, a tiny cake with a candle, anything to make it fun for him and the entire family.

When he wets the bed, have him change his own bedding. No lectures—do not scold! Have him put his wet clothing and sheets in the laundry room. Remember, his progress will be uneven. At first, he will have a dry night and many wet nights. Over a period of weeks, this will change and he will wet only occasionally. Keep him on the program until he has been dry for several weeks.

TEMPER TANTRUMS*

Many parents seem to be troubled with children who have frequent temper tantrums. Telling the child that he cannot have or do something often results in loud whining, yelling, running, hitting, and throwing things. This display may last from a minute or two up to half an hour's harassment of the parent. There are perhaps some good days, but on a bad day tantrums may occur two or three times. Tantrums can occur in the supermarket, at the playground, or in the home of a relative. Some children seem to have a sixth sense about selecting the most embarrassing situations in which to stage their performances. It comes to a point for some parents where they are afraid to say "No" to their child. Collect data each day for a week to get a baseline rate (see Chapter 5).

The basic idea is to teach the child that temper tantrums and whining will no longer "work." Because the procedure relies mainly upon the use of Time Out, you should reread

* The author wishes to thank Brian Danaher for his assistance in field-testing these procedures.

Chapter 8 before proceeding. Arrange for a conference with your four-year-old. Both parents must be present; *if one parent refuses to cooperate, then the program will probably not work.*

"You are a big boy now and can do lots of big boy things. One problem though is a worry to your mother and me. It seems a lot of times when we say 'No' you get pretty upset and do lots of yelling and whining. I think you can learn to stop doing that; we will help you practice. Each time you have a temper tantrum, we will say, 'OK, three minutes of Time Out.' Then you go into the bathroom. I will set this timer for three minutes. When it goes off, you come out. OK?"

Remember that Time Out means three minutes alone in the bathroom with the door closed. The child is timed out at the start of each tantrum behavior. If he does not go into Time Out when he is supposed to, he is told that he must spend an extra minute in TO for not minding. The kitchen timer is set so the child can hear it ring when TO is over, and under no circumstances does anyone talk to the child during TO. If the child is noisy when the timer rings, the timer is reset for one minute and the child remains in TO. This is done as many times as is needed until the child is quiet when the timer rings. The child must clean up any mess he made while he was in TO.

It is also a good idea to use the gold star chart and provide gold stars for each compliance. If you say "No" and he minds you with no whines and temper tantrums, say, "Hey, I said 'No' and you acted like a big boy! That's great! Here's a gold star for your chart." The temper tantrums should reduce by at least half by the end of two or three weeks. If not, then consult a trained behavior modifier or pediatrician for assistance.

THE MIDNIGHT INTRUDER

Many parents find it is a warm, pleasant feeling to have their two-year-old occasionally slip into their bed in the middle of

108

the night. Certainly this is not a "problem" behavior. Some difficulties seem to arise, however, when the parents decide that it is time to teach the child to stay in his own bed. The following procedure seems to work well, and is a nice example of the simplicity of some social learning programs.

Be sure both parents agree that they want privacy. Both parents then explain the program to their child. "Now that you are a big boy, it is time for you to learn to stay in your own bed at night. When you forget and climb in our bed, we are just going to take you back to your own bed. If you stay in your own bed all night, then one of us will climb into *your* bed in the morning and read stories for fifteen minutes. OK? If you climb in our bed, no stories. If you stay in your bed, then we'll come there in the morning for storytime."

If the child cries when you return him to his bed, ignore him and let him cry it out. He should be able to learn to stay in bed after three or four more attempts to invade yours.

WHINING

Most children whine once or twice a day to get attention, or over some minor injury, or when you leave. But a child that whines once an hour or more may present a behavior problem. If you want to reduce your child's rate of whining, you must teach the child that whining will no longer "work." To do this, you will need to change the way that you respond when he whines.

Buy a box of gold stars, and tape a gold star chart to the refrigerator door. Explain the program to your child. "You are a big boy now and can do a lot of things. There is a problem, though, that bothers me. The problem is that you whine a number of times each day. I'm going to help you practice so this won't happen so often. See the chart here on the door? Each time you whine, I'm going to put a mark in the box. Each day has its own box. See, here is for today. If you go a whole hour with no whines, then you get to have a gold star in the box. How many stars do you think you will get today?"

When the child has gone for an hour with no whines, say, "This has really been nice. You haven't whined for an hour! What a big boy you are! Should I put the gold star up or do you want to do it?" Give the child the star even if the child has not been around you. Be as enthusiastic as you can. Show your approval: Give a kiss and hug as well as saying, "Good boy!"

Every time the child whines, say, "OK, three minutes of Time Out." Explain to him beforehand that this will happen and demonstrate Time Out. Remember that Time Out means three minutes alone in the bathroom with the door closed, and under no circumstances does anyone talk to the child during TO. A kitchen timer is set so that the child knows when TO is over.

If the child does not comply with the request that he go into TO, he is informed that he must spend an extra minute for not going alone. If the child is noisy when the timer rings, the timer is reset for one minute, and the child remains in TO. This happens every time the child is noisy when the timer rings. The child must also clean up any mess he made while he was in TO.

After a week or two it won't be necessary to use the gold stars so often. By this time, let the child trade stars for extra reading time or extra snuggling time before bed. The whines should reduce by *at least half* their usual rate at the end of two or three weeks.

TO BED OR NOT TO BED

You tuck him in bed, kiss him goodnight, and what happens? Five minutes later you hear tiny footsteps in the hall, a little voice calling. . . . If this happens almost every night, you may want to change these behaviors.

Begin by explaining the program to your child after you tuck him in. "You just went to the potty and had a drink of

110

water. Is there anything else you need right now? OK? From now on I want you to stay in your bed after I tuck you in. If you get out of bed, then you go into Time Out for three minutes. If you stay in your bed and are quiet, then tomorrow night you and I will have a special treat. I will read to you for ten minutes before you go to bed. If you get out of bed, then you get Time Out and no bedtime story. If you stay in bed, then tomorrow night is storytime."

If the child lays in bed and asks for you, and you are sure he is okay, then ignore him. When he gets out of bed, use Time Out. Do not lecture: The first time simply take him by the hand and lead him to the bathroom door. "Time Out means you sit in here for three minutes. When the timer goes off, you can come out and go directly to bed." Set the kitchen timer so the child can hear it ring when TO is over. Under no circumstances should anyone talk to the child during Time Out. If the child is noisy in the bathroom, reset the timer for an extra minute. "Yelling means you stay longer." The child must clean up any mess he made during Time Out.

The next night, give the child a thirty-minute warning. "Half an hour to bedtime, better pick up your things and get ready." If the child stayed in bed the previous night, even if he cried all night long, say, "You stayed in bed last night. You were so good we get to read a story as soon as you are in bed. Are you all ready?"

If the child didn't stay in bed the night before, say, "We don't get a bedtime story tonight. Think you can stay in bed tonight?" Do not lecture or scold.

By the end of two or three weeks this program should have the child staying in bed almost every night.

If your problem is a relatively simple one, you've probably been able to use the procedures described in this chapter to reduce the problem by at least half. The combination of gold stars and Time Out used for many of these problems should work for you within the first two weeks. If not, then *you may wish to contact a licensed psychologist who is trained in social learning procedures, or your family pediatrician.*

If you go on simply applying the procedures you've already been given, you will find that within a week or two, your child is no longer interested in gold stars. At this point, it may be necessary to negotiate with the child so that his gold stars earn him back-up reinforcers. For example, each of his gold stars might earn him five minutes of reading time each evening. For more complete information, you might refer to Section II.

Key Ideas in Chapter 10

Pick out specific target behaviors you want to change.
Explain the program to the child.
Do not nag or scold.
Do not argue or debate.
Both parents must participate.
Consult a professional behavior modifier and/or your pediatrician if any program described here does not work.

Section IV

APPLICATIONS
TO MORE COMPLICATED
MANAGEMENT PROBLEMS

This section details, step by step, the application of social learning procedures to changing the more complicated problem behaviors of young children. The first chapter describes procedures found effective for working with young boys and girls who steal. The second chapter details behavior change programs for aggressive children. We began working with these two types of conduct problems in 1965 with a series of NIMH grants sponsored by the Section on Crime and Delinquency. Their sponsorship in no way implies an endorsement of the materials presented in this section. It does, however, emphasize their concern, and our own, for developing procedures to apply to the younger child who is developing conduct problem behaviors. Follow-up studies of such children indicate that their eventual adjustment as adults may be tenuous (Robins, 1966). Even as adults they are likely to continue to have severe problems in their relationships to other people and to the world of work.

   The material in this section describes the steps to be followed by parents working with professional social learning therapists. Out of efforts to teach parents of extremely aggressive boys to manage their own children have come a number of research reports (Patterson, 1969; Patterson, Cobb, and Ray, 1971, 1973; Patterson, Ray, and Shaw, 1968). The clinical work was accompanied by intensive observations made in the homes of these families. These data provide the basis for some understanding of the process by which children and families become involved in such behaviors. Many of the papers describing this long series of analyses have already been published (Patterson and Cobb, 1971b; Patterson, Littman, and Bricker, 1967; Patterson and Reid, 1970) and such work continues at the present time. As yet, only one paper has been published describing the outcome of our efforts to work with children who steal (Phillips and Wolf, 1968).

The earlier book, *Living with Children,* contained chapters describing procedures for working with withdrawn, dependent-immature, and fearful children. Since publishing that book, we have carried out only a minimal amount of clinical research; for this reason, no attempt was made to include chapters relevant to these problem areas in *Families.* Those interested in these problems should refer to the earlier volume.

Chapters 11 and 12 would, of course, be required reading for parents who have children displaying high rates of aggressive behaviors or stealing; they are in fact required reading for parents who are referred to the Family Center at the Oregon Research Institute. These chapters were written explicitly for those parents who have aggressive children or children who steal. They are designed to teach the parents how to function as a colleague in the treatment process. However, these chapters also describe examples of planning and carrying out programs. The details of the steps involved and the overall continuity of the programs employed should give *all* parents a more detailed account of how one goes about designing and carrying out intervention programs.

11

The Child Who Steals

> Even when everything is nice for him, he'll just up and steal something.
> He's not a bad boy, he just takes things.
> He's a sneaky kid.

It is probably true that at one time or another almost everyone has stolen something. Taking something that belongs to another person without first asking their permission is part of the normal play pattern of a two- or three-year-old child. By the age of five or six, most children have learned to stop stealing and less than one child in ten continues to steal at a high rate (Morris, 1956). Just for the sake of discussion, let's say that a child who steals more than once a month represents a problem. Each parent sets his own standards in these matters. However, if a child is stealing even small things at this rate, his behavior will eventually come to the attention of the community. When this happens, he will be labeled as deviant and his relations with teachers and peers will perhaps be altered to his detriment.

Stealing, Lying, and Wandering

We have found a relationship between aggressive behavior and stealing. If a child has one problem, he has a 50-50 chance of also having the other. *The problems which almost invariably accompany stealing are lying and wandering.*

The three problems which seem to go together are 1_____, 2_____, and 3_____. It is easy to see why these things go together. As the parent slowly comes to believe his child is a thief, he confronts the child whenever anything is missing. There are endless family "trial" scenes. In each instance, the child practices his skill at deception. Most of the children with whom we have worked can look an adult straight in the eye while telling the most outrageous lies.

The parent is caught in a trap constructed by our society. When considering adult thieves, the assumption is always "innocent until proven guilty." In many instances, there were no eyewitnesses to their child's thievery. The fact that the fountain pen disappeared from the neighboring child's desk, only to reappear in their son's pocket is mysterious, to say the least. No one saw it in its flight from one location to the other; therefore, the case cannot be proven. Indeed, it *may be*, as he says, that a girlfriend really did put the pen there; and how was he to know she was a thief?

It all seems plausible, and many parents are truly confused. Many times they are pretty sure the child stole something, but they cannot prove it. The fact that the child becomes a highly skilled liar adds further to the problem. Therefore, the first step in changing this behavior is to change the rules: Redefine what is meant by stealing. Over a two-week period, count every new object which turns up as "stolen." Each time he "finds" something, tally it as "steal." We dealt with one child who claimed he found two transistor radios in one week! Anything which he says was "given" to him is tallied in the same way. If the teacher said lunch money was taken from another child's desk, then count it as 4_____. If you even "feel" that you are missing money from your purse, tally it as "steal." If some of the

1. stealing   2. lying   3. wandering   4. steal

cookies are missing after you told all the children "hands off," then count it. In this new game, you do not have to 5_____ that your child stole something. It is up to him to learn to stay out of situations in which his behavior will look suspicious. *It is no longer necessary to prove that he stole.* It is true that you will occasionally punish him for something which he did not do. While this temporary disruption of justice may offend your sensibilities, it is necessary for the few weeks needed to train your child to stop his thievery.

The third component, "wandering," refers to the fact that many young thieves have a great deal of unsupervised time for themselves. This child tends not to come directly home from school. Some of them wander off the schoolyard at recess time and simply "forget" to return. Similarly, they tend to disappear after supper and return hours later. The practiced thief tends to use these unsupervised times to explore such things as stores, parked cars, and other persons' homes. Often these forays are in the company of other children who are equally skilled. The child asserts that it is his right to spend his time as he pleases. If you choose to quiz him about his activities during these times, he simply lies to you so you are again effectively checkmated. As his expeditions are reinforced by peers, they tend to increase in scope and duration. This in turn is accompanied by a rising tide of protests and accusations from neighbors, storekeepers, and eventually the police. Even though the parent knows that his child did not really do all the things of which he stands accused, he gradually begins to accept the idea that sometimes his child is in fact a thief. Because of our society's concern over property, and the loss of it, eventual institutionalization is a very real possibility.

Certainly an older child should have a certain amount of freedom to explore his neighborhood and his community. However, it is also reasonable that the child be required to let his parents know where he is going and when to expect his

5. prove

return. The child who steals has generally not been taught to do either of these things. For this reason, we label his un-supervised time as 6_____.

A Behavior Change Program for Stealing

The treatment program found effective for these children (Phillips and Wolf, 1968) *is focused upon a point system covering all three problem behaviors: lying, wandering, and stealing.* If there are problems with social aggression, these behaviors are also included in the program. As a first step, it is important to communicate the fact to the child that the rules are about to change.

"Tim, we are going to try and help you with your steal-ing problem. From now on, every time you steal it will cost you an hour's work on the same day. If someone calls and even says that they think you stole something, it will cost you an hour. If you find something, don't bring it home because it will count as stealing. The same for people giving you things—don't accept them. Anything missing around here will be counted as 'steal.' It will be up to you to stay away from situations where it looks like you might be stealing."

Many parents are reluctant, at first, to take such a hard line. They say that their child's brothers and sisters or children at school might accuse him of stealing just to get him in trouble. This does seem like a reasonable concern but this has not been a problem with the thirty families with whom we have worked. Interestingly enough, very few of the children report the program to be unfair after they have been involved for a week or two.

6. wandering

Assuming there were no problems at school or with social aggression, a simple contract for Tim might be like this one. (Note: Tim's regular bedtime is 8:30.)

Name _Tim_								
Behavior (points possible)	M	T	W	T	F	S	S	M
No stealing (4)	4	0	0	4	0	4	4	0
No lying (2)	2	0	2	0	2	2	0	0
No wandering (4)	4	4	0	4	0	0	0	4
Total	10	4	2	8	2	6	4	4

Consequences: 10 pts. – 9:00 bedtime, plus dessert
8 pts. – 8:30 bedtime, plus dessert
6 pts. – 8:00 bedtime
4 pts. – 7:30 bedtime
2 pts. – 7:30 bedtime, wash dishes
0 pts. – 7:30 bedtime, wash dishes 2 days
TO for wandering; 1 hr. housework for stealing

The first five days of data were collected without Tim's knowledge. The data showed he had some very good days and some very bad days. The first day after the program had been introduced (Saturday), Tim earned four points for not stealing and two points for not lying. He did return home a half hour later than he was expected, so he lost four points for wandering and had to spend five minutes in Time Out. That gave him a total of six points, and he had to go to bed a half hour earlier than his usual bedtime.

During the negotiation session, Tim and his parents agreed that he could lose points for wandering if he did not report to his mother right after school to tell her where he would be, who he would be with, and when he would be home. If Tim's parents decided to check up on him and he was not where he was supposed to be, he lost points for lying.

On the third day of the program (Monday), Tim's teacher called to say that money had been taken from her desk. Tim had treated several children to toys and candy during lunch hour. Tim denied that he had bought anything for other children. He therefore lost points for stealing and lying. He had to do one hour of housework that evening and be in bed by 7:30.

During the weeks that followed, the contract was changed a number of times. Eventually the parents added "Doing Chores (2)," "Doing Homework (2)," and reduced the points for "Not Stealing" (3), "Not Lying" (1), and "Not Wandering" (2). The possible seventy points per week became the means by which Tim earned his allowance.

After numerous wandering and several more stealing episodes, he eventually stopped doing these things. During follow-up, the parents no longer used the point system, but he did have to earn his allowance by doing chores and keeping his room clean. Every month or two, he would come home late and promptly find himself scrubbing floors or doing dishes. Like most children, he simply needed to know that the rules still applied.

Key Ideas in Chapter 11

Stealing, lying, and wandering go together as problems.
Don't try to prove he steals.
Use the point system for each problem.

12

The Aggressive Child

> You just don't know when he is going to blow up.
> He just keeps things stirred up all the time.
> It is impossible to get him to do anything.
> He is stubborn, just like his father.
> He acts as if no one likes him.
> He has a terrible temper.

What is meant by the phrase "aggressive child"? Other children hit, tease, and sometimes refuse to obey adult requests. Actually, the aggressive child does what most children do, but at a higher rate and in situations where it is not acceptable. Most children do not hit as often as once a day; they do not tease at the rate of once an hour. They obey most parental requests and demands. *Hitting, noncompliance, and "bugging" are behaviors displayed by most children sometimes; however, the aggressive child distinguishes himself by displaying them at higher* 1_____ .

The aggressive child teases his younger brother, hits, and yells in such a variety of settings that the parents become confused. "You just never know what he is going to do." He may have a temper outburst in the midst of an otherwise

1. rates

pleasant scene, such as a birthday party or at a store. He may tease his sister while on a shopping trip or noncomply in the presence of visitors. The aggressive child displays his high rate behaviors in a wider variety of 2_____ than do other children.

The Aggressive Child Within the Family

When such a pattern of high rate responding develops, it is likely to cause changes within the total family system. The brothers and sisters may get caught up in a pattern of using teasing, yelling, and hitting at high rates. The parents can also find themselves spanking more often. The children and the parents tend to label the aggressive child as "bad," and he comes to think of himself in this way. When asked why he does these things he cannot give an explanation; usually he blames others for forcing him to act in this way. "They bugged me so I had to hit 'em."

If a crisis arises, a displeasure occurs, or he is momentarily blocked from obtaining a reward, he attacks. With such a child it is difficult to conceive of forming a close relationship. In the school he is avoided by other children. He is disliked by other people (Moore, 1967). Not only does he inflict pain upon other people, but he tends not to reinforce other children or adults. It is indeed difficult to like such a person. He feels that he is rejected and disliked, as indeed he is. It is an odd fact that in spite of his skill in disrupting a whole household or classroom, he is not very sure of himself. He teaches others to dislike him.

His attacks create a pervading unpleasant mood. He also creates a situation in which both parents and siblings are changed. The brothers and sisters are provided with a highly skilled model for teasing, hitting, and noncompliance. In addition, they are placed in a learning situation where they must learn to retaliate in some manner. An attack increases the likelihood that at some time in the future the victim will

2. settings

124

retaliate (Patterson and Reid, 1970). If the older brother is hitting and teasing his younger sister, she will learn to return the attacks in some form. Then *two* persons are behaving in a manner which will disrupt the whole household. Unless the parents find some means of handling the attacks of the aggressive child, other children in the family will almost certainly devise some means of retaliating. Attacks breed 3_____. The aggressive child will respond to these counterattacks with yet further attacks which escalate the conflicts within the home.

The adults within the family are also drawn into this escalating interchange. Even if they believe that it is good for boys to learn to fight and tease, they will find that the noise level exceeds their tolerance level. As the children increase their rates of attacks and counterattacks, the parents resort to yelling, nagging, and spanking. All of these will temporarily shut off the conflict. This slight interruption in chaos 4_____ both parents for yelling, nagging, and spanking. We now have a situation in which the behavior of one person—the aggressive child—sets up a chain reaction which eventually involves all members of the family. The family is a social system in that what one person does influences what other members do.

As more family members get drawn into the conflict, making increasing use of punishment, they probably begin to develop feelings about the family which are increasingly negative. And it is probably difficult to use positive social reinforcement with people who are making you miserable. This means that members of these families may end up being forced to use primarily painful consequences to control each other's behavior. At the end of such an escalating process, there is little love in such homes.

Aggressive Behavior is Learned

The reinforcer for aggressive behaviors is usually not praise, social approval, points, or money. Hitting is strengthened

3. attacks   4. reinforces

because it "works" in removing aversive stimuli. The process is similar to that which strengthens parental yelling, nagging, and scolding. The sister's teasing is an 5 _____ stimulus. The aggressive child has learned that if he hits her, it will 6 _____ her teasing. The behavior that is strengthened here is 7 _____ . This increases the likelihood that he will hit in the future. He learns that hitting "works" in turning off a wide variety of unpleasant situations. A family need only allow the hitter to be reinforced in this manner to produce a high rate of hitting. The same child usually learns that a temper tantrum is an effective means of training parents to stop asking him to do things he doesn't want to do.

Why do some families have high rate hitters and not others? While it may be that there are related genetic or physiological differences among children, there are as yet no studies which firmly establish these differences as causing aggressive behavior. On the other hand, it has been shown that an amazing variety of aggressive children can be trained to stop hitting. Retarded children, brain-damaged children, adolescents, and even autistic children can be trained to lower their hitting rates.

The parents of aggressive children do not necessarily have "psychiatric problems," nor are they "stupid" or "bad" people. Many of them have already reared several children very effectively. Parents of the aggressive child do have one thing in common, though; they do not provide consistent consequences for hitting or noncompliance. They will occasionally punish hitting, teasing, or noncompliant behavior, but more often than not the behaviors are reinforced. Some parents have been told that their child is retarded, brain-damaged, or emotionally disturbed, with the implication that limits and structure would be "bad" for the child. Some children have been cared for by baby sitters or grandparents who have provided no consequences for such behaviors. Some parents have simply been so busy with the world outside the family that they have not taken the time to track the

5. aversive   6. stop   7. hitting

child's behavior and provide consequences. The thing that they all have in common is that they do not track these hitting, teasing, and noncompliant behaviors, nor do they provide a 8_____ when the behaviors occur.

Again, it should be stressed that these children are not born 9 _____. They do not have something wrong with them. They have been trained to be high rate hitters by members of their own 10_____. Parents from all walks of life can accidentally slip into the pattern which will produce this kind of training. Most importantly, the family can retrain such a child to 11_____ his rates of hitting, teasing, and noncompliance.

This does not mean that the appropriate goal is necessarily that of teaching him never to hit. In our society, it might be necessary for him to be able to fight back when he is attacked. The goal, specifically, is to teach him to hit at a lower rate, and in appropriate situations.

PINPOINTING AND CHANGING NONCOMPLIANCE

Each aggressive child seems to have learned a slightly different pattern of aggressive behaviors. Some hit only their little brothers, others hit everyone, including their parents. Some tease, run away from school and home, steal, and light fires. Some are noisy and hyperactive, while others are silent and rather withdrawn. Each aggressive child is somewhat unique, and it is up to the family to pinpoint the specific problems which define the child's aggressive behaviors.

With these children it is wise to *begin with one problem behavior at a time*. Do not select the problem that "bothers you the most" as a point of beginning. *Practice on relatively trivial problems first*. It is also important to select a behavior that occurs at a fairly high rate, that is, at least once an hour. Learning to deal with this relatively simple problem requires that you practice the basic skills which will be used to deal with more complex aspects of aggression. "Noncompliance"

8. punishment, consequence   9. bad   10. family   11. reduce

is a good problem behavior for your first program. Noncompliance means that the parent makes a request and the child does not comply. Most aggressive children display high rates of these behaviors.

Pinpointing Noncompliance

Each child has different ways of operating. You must observe your child for a day or two to see what his noncompliance technique is. For example, he may be an "instant exploder." If he is asked to carry out the garbage, he responds with loud yells and informs the world that it is definitely not his turn. When does his sister do anything? People are always hassling him.

There is also the "smiling footdragger": He responds in his most cheerful voice, "Sure, Mom, right away." Somehow the garbage does not get taken out right then, nor later. Unless his mother follows him about the house and nags, he just "forgets." Some of them are three-, four-, even eight-nag children. It depends upon how well they have trained their parents. A true maestro can get his parents up to ten nags and still comply only once in a while. They find it is easier to do it themselves than to try to out-nag him.

The request should be stated specifically: "I'd like the garbage taken out in the next thirty minutes." Specify the amount of 12_____ he has to comply. If the child does not do it in the specified time, it is a "noncomply." If you have to argue or ask him twice, it is a noncomply. If he is doing something he really enjoys, give him time to become disengaged: "As soon as that TV program is over, please take the garbage out." For some behaviors, you will not, of course, tolerate any delay: "Stop that teasing right now, both of you." If the teasing continues, that is a noncomply.

If the behavior occurs at a high rate (two or more times per hour), you might select just one or two hours each day during which you will make your count. During that time

12. time

128

make sure that both parents give him several requests. If his noncomplies are less than once an hour, you might decide to count occurrences during the whole day. 13 _____ parents should participate in this counting. Some fathers attempt to bow out and leave it to the mother. Don't let this happen. Your program will almost certainly fail if both parents are not participating.

Take a data card from the appendix of this book and tape it on the refrigerator door. *Identify the specific behaviors which define noncompliance for your child.*

DATA CARD			
Name___Eric_____			
Behavior: _Noncomply: argues, doesn't do what his asked, takes too long, too sloppy_			
Day	Number of Behaviors	Time Interval	Rate
Mon	TMK II	3:30 – 4:30	7/hr
Tues	I	3:30 – 4:30	1/hr
Wed	TMK	3:30 – 4:20	6/hr
Thurs	TMK III	3:30 – 4:30	8/hr
Fri	TMK I	3:30 – 4:10	9/hr

13. Both

Calculate your rate on the basis of hours or minutes. In either case, Eric, the boy in the example above, is turning out high rates of noncompliant behavior. The parents should collect a baseline of at least 14_____ days of data in order to obtain a stable starting point. In spite of the temptation to "get going," do not rush this phase.

Reinforcing for Compliance

Eric was ten years old and a practiced monster. He not only hit his younger sister, but had completely alienated himself from children in the neighborhood as well. He was so bossy that other children avoided playing with him. He was likely to settle disagreements with an all-out attack. At home he made derogatory remarks about his mother and his sister. He was large enough and aggressive enough so that his mother felt she could not handle him. The father claimed that when he was home Eric was well-behaved; observations in the home showed that this, in fact, was the case.

Eric was so skilled at noncompliance that neither the father nor the mother asked him to do anything. As is the case for most aggressive boys, both parents had been trained to believe that Eric *could not* mind or do chores. After four days of baseline observation it was clear that he provided about one noncomply every ten minutes. Even on his best day, which was 15_____ , his noncompliance rate was 16 _____ per hour. At the end of baseline the parents discussed the data with him and explained the contract.

"Eric, we have been counting your 'not minding' for the last few days." He hardly indicated that he had heard. "Ma, can I go outside now?" The father pointed at the chair and said, "You sit down for a minute, then you can go out." Then Eric, still standing, answered, "Why should I? Look at

14. three   15. Tuesday   16. one

130

Lauri; she never does anything around here. Little six-year-old, doll-sister, never has to do anything. Why is she so special, anyhow?"

The mother avoided this sidetracking maneuver and stayed on the topic. "Starting right now we are going to help you practice minding. Lauri is going to practice not bugging you. I think you will find that programs are sort of fun; the way that they work is that you get a point each time you mind when your father or I ask you to do something. For example, if I say, 'Please come to supper in the next couple of minutes,' and you do it, then you get a point. We keep track of the points right here." She points to the data card.

Eric is sitting staring out the window, as if he does not hear. His father is becoming slightly irritated at this. "You can earn points every day for doing what you are told. You have to help us by letting us know what you want to work for. What do you want to use the points for?" Eric quietly whispers, "I don't want no points for nothin'."

He refuses to negotiate. This has the desired effect of completely unraveling his father. Before the father can move in with his heavy artillery and "solve the problem," the mother continues.

"Well, you can let us know later on what you wish to do with the points. For the next three days, we'll just practice giving points and taking them away so you can see how it works. OK, let's have one practice to see if we all understand. This is for real; and you will earn a point and a nickel. Eric, please turn the TV set down for me before you go outside."

Eric slowly drags out of the room and touches the volume knob before going outside. His mother says, "OK, that is a point. Thank you, Eric."

In this discussion, Eric tried to sabotage the negotiations and direct the discussion elsewhere. He did this by attacking Lauri and attempting to get the parents to defend the child management procedures they used with her. He also refused to negotiate the back-up reinforcers for the point program. Many aggressive children approach their first session in this manner. Ignore the words they use, and attempt to immediately provide a reinforcer for whatever level of compliance you can get from them. In this case, Eric barely touched the volume knob, so his first response was hardly satisfactory by most standards. However, that is where he is at the present time. During the first day, even minimal compliance is reinforced.

Do not lecture when he noncomplies. Just record it and ignore it. Emphasize your pleasure at the minimal compliance you do obtain: "Eric, you earned five points today for minding. That was a good beginning. You lost two when you forgot and didn't mind. How many points do you think you'll earn tomorrow? Have you decided what you want to earn with your points?"

After several days of practice using points, Eric decided he'd like to earn the right to stay up later at night. It was decided that if he got three or more points, he could stay up thirty minutes later that evening. If his point score was minus three or worse, then he was to go to bed thirty minutes earlier. He was also given to understand that there was to be much more talk about these agreements. He would be given opportunities then to make changes in what he worked for.

Both parents might select one hour during the day when they will search for and find some aspect of the child's behavior that can be reinforced. You might agree between yourselves as to what the target behaviors might be; they should, of course, include "comply," but also might include things like "acting more grown-up," "being less noisy," "being helpful," or "playing appropriately." During that hour try to dispense five to ten social reinforcers of different kinds for any of these behaviors. As reinforcers you might use 17_____, 18_____, 19_____, or 20_____.

17, 18, 19, 20. Could be praise, smiling, touching, kissing, participating in what he is doing, etc.

TO for Noncompliance

After the reinforcement programs are underway, you are in a position to introduce TO for noncompliance. Carefully controlled laboratory research has shown that for many aggressive children it is necessary to supplement the effects of reinforcement by the use of TO (Wahler, 1967; Walker, Mattson, and Buckley, 1969). Many parents hesitate to introduce it for retraining their aggressive child because they are afraid that they cannot follow through in carrying it out. However, it is an important aspect of the training program.

"Eric, you have been doing pretty well on the program, but you still forget to mind. We are going to start using Time Out to help you remember. It will also help your father and me to stop nagging and scolding as much as we do. From now on, if you forget to mind when I ask you to do something, then you go to Time Out. That means that you go and sit in the bathroom for five minutes. When we tell you to go in, we will set the timer for five minutes. When the timer goes off, you can come out."

Eric is scowling at this point. "Go ahead and put me in there; I like to be away from all you creeps, anyway. I like to be by myself. I like it in the toilet. Go on, put me in there right now, see if I care! It ain't going to work."

The mother ignores this and goes on, "If you come out before the timer goes off, you have to stay in one minute extra. Or if you talk to anyone while you are in there, that costs an extra minute, too."

Eric does not look at her or his father. "Aw, what a crummy thing. Just like a jail. What about Lauri, huh? What about her? Does she go in there too."

But remember to use TO 21_____ time the noncompliance occurs. When Eric was jumping up and down on the couch an hour later, his father told him to go to TO, and then set the timer for five minutes.

21. every

133

Eric ran outside and stood on the sidewalk, yelling at his father, "I ain't going in there; I'm going to run away. It's just a crummy jail in that house!"

The father was getting angry, but said, "That is one minute extra for running out here. It is another minute for yelling at me. You'd better come in and get it over with. It is another minute for each one that you stay out here." With that, he closed the door and went back into the house.

Eric circled the house for a few minutes, occasionally stopped to make a face in the window, but eventually came in. "OK. Five minutes, that's all. Besides, I like it in there."

His father announced, "No, it is not five minutes; you were outside for eight minutes, you have an extra minute for yelling at me, one for running outside, and three for making faces through the window. That is eighteen altogether."

Eric began to yell and kick at the door as he went in. His father closed the door and said calmly, "That is one more for yelling and another for kicking the door."

When Eric had been in there a few minutes, he began to shout, "Is it time yet?" When no one answered, he began to cry. At this point his mother became upset and stated loudly enough for Eric to hear that perhaps he should be let out. A short time later he burst out of the bathroom and announced that he was all through. The father returned him to TO and added another minute. Each yell that followed cost him more time, but the father no longer announced each one. When, at the end of thirty minutes, he came out, the father told him, again, that each yell, kick, and running out of the room had cost him. Some parents find it necessary to actually hold the door the first few times. If this happens, make sure you do not talk to the child while he is in TO.

By the end of the first week the combination of TO with the point program and social reinforcement seemed to be having some effect. Both parents reported that things were changing and that home was now occasionally pleasant. Surprisingly enough, Eric acted as if he were happier!

The point programs were changed several times so that by the second week he was working for five or six days in order to earn the fifty points necessary for his father to take him trout fishing. The trip was a huge success. The father had previously noted his tendency to criticize Eric in all kinds of situations and made a special effort to keep these comments in check. He found Eric to be genuinely interested in learning some of the many skills necessary to become a trout fisherman. While other trips were planned, Eric next elected to earn one hundred points for an inexpensive secondhand TV set for his room. The parents found that as the programs progressed they began asking Eric to assume more responsibilities about the house, including sharing in the dishwashing in the evenings. Eric shared the responsibility with his mother for one week and Lauri did them the following week. Eric's progress is described in the figure below.

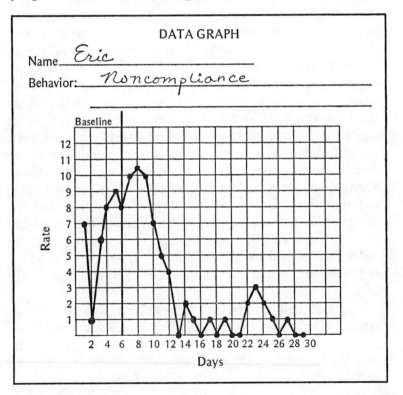

DATA GRAPH

Name: Eric

Behavior: Noncompliance

As the figure shows, the first week produced no change; in fact, the first 22_____ days of data looked worse than the baseline. It is also clear that Eric is far from being perfect; but then again, the parents did not require perfection, only progress. On the sixteenth day of training the grandparents arrived for the holidays. Both of them objected to the use of TO and points. Their contribution to the family is recorded on the graph.

At the end of the second week, the parents felt that things were going well enough to consider beginning new programs.

CHANGING OTHER AGGRESSIVE BEHAVIORS

After having been successful with the noncompliance program, Eric's parents were slightly encouraged. At least they had proved to themselves that they really could help Eric change his behavior. However, it was also clear that the most difficult problems still remained. He and Lauri were constantly bugging and teasing each other; major battles occurred several times a day. Some of these battles got the whole family embroiled, and bad feelings remained for hours afterward. He seemed to go out of his way to make everyone uncomfortable. For example, he would stand behind his mother as she was talking to someone, saying, "Mom, Mom, Mom, Mom, Mom . . ." until she stopped what she was doing and responded to him. He would still explode and throw things or hit without warning at home and in the school and the neighborhood. Eric was thought to be "dangerous" by other parents and by teachers. Many of the families in the neighborhood would not allow their children to play with Eric.

About half of the children who show high rates of aggressive behaviors and noncompliance at home have similar problems at school. Eric was no exception. Even though he

22. three

136

was in the second grade, he was reading at an early first-grade level. He was constantly disrupting the class—clowning around, running about the room, and laughing and talking in a loud voice to his neighbors. When he was asked to do something by the teacher, he was very likely to ignore her or talk back to her. He would seldom complete his assignments, and when he did, the work was sloppy and often incorrect. Once every week or so he would have an explosion in which he would attack other children with anything at hand. The danger to the other children understandably frightened his teachers.

Contracting with Brothers and Sisters

Eric's behavior was only part of this problem. His little sister Lauri is an important piece to this puzzle. She had an uncanny knack of knowing just what buttons to push to set her brother off. While things might start out as "play," it is amazing how often games turned into arguments, running shaded into pushing, and teasing led to hitting. Certainly it cannot be said that Lauri "started" all of these battles. It is just that she was a necessary component for most of them. Extensive observations made in homes of both problem and non-problem families show that this is not unusual. The member of the family most likely to trigger aggressive behaviors is the younger sister or younger brother (Patterson and Cobb, 1971a). Lauri was an attractive young lady, four years of age, and practiced in the wiles necessary to stop her father in mid-stride. By saying something cute and delivering an impish grin, she could interrupt her father in the middle of his saying "No," and cause him to forget what he was trying to do. Because she was so young, the parents were reluctant to involve her in a training program. After all, she was only four, and "their last baby."

While it was conceivable that Eric's behavior could be changed without directly changing Lauri's, it would have been very inefficient—clumsy and time-consuming—especially since Lauri would have had to learn some other means of relating to her brother eventually. Certainly from Eric's viewpoint, justice would be better served by a program which did something about this younger sister who was always bugging him.

Name _Eric_							
Behavior (points possible)	M	T	W	T	F	S	S
Being pleasant (+2)							
Getting dressed w/o help (+2)							
Room neat, bed made (+3)							
Minding parents (+1)							
Asking permission to leave (+2)							
Doing chores (+4)							
Teasing, bugging, yelling (-2)							
Hitting, grabbing, shoving (-3)							
Not minding (-1)							
Breaking things (-2)							
Total							

Consequences: +3 pts. — treat for afternoon snack
+5 pts. — may use bike, leave yard
+7 pts. — can stay up 30 min. later
Teasing, yelling, grabbing, shoving, hitting, not minding — 5 min. TO.

The next step involved setting up a contract which would apply both to Eric and Lauri. The first contract did not involve any of the problems at school, but did identify major points in the problems at home. An effort was made to find those behaviors that would apply to both Eric and Lauri and also to find back-up reinforcers appropriate to both.

Each time that Eric or Lauri was pleasant, the parents would label the behavior: "That's nice. You two are playing well together. You both get a point." The mother would then walk over and put a mark in the box for each child. Neither Eric nor Lauri could completely dress themselves. They had

Name *Lauri*							
Behavior (points possible)	M	T	W	T	F	S	S
Being pleasant (+2)							
Getting dressed w/o help (+2)							
Room neat, bed made (+3)							
Minding parents (+1)							
Asking permission to leave (+2)							
Doing chores (+4)							
Teasing, bugging, yelling (-2)							
Hitting, grabbing, shoving (-3)							
Not minding (-1)							
Breaking things (-2)							
Total							

Consequences: *+3 pts. – treat for afternoon snack*
+5 pts. – may use bike and leave yard
+7 pts. – can stay up 15 min. later
Teasing, yelling, grabbing, shoving,
hitting, not minding – 5 min. T.O.

trained their mother to believe that they were both completely helpless. While the mother still laid out their clothes for them, she made an extra effort to be very reinforcing if they made any moves to dress themselves. In the first session with Eric, he managed to get his pants and shirt on by himself, and the mother promptly reinforced this: "That's very good, Eric; you get one point for that." She also made similar evaluations for the way in which the two children made their beds on the first few days. In fact, on the first day neither child made the bed nor cleaned up the room. The mother commented as she walked down the hall that nobody got any points today because the room was still a mess and neither bed had been made. Lauri seized upon this opportunity to do her brother one better and quickly shoved clothes and toys under the bed and draped the bedcover over the sheets and blankets underneath. The mother commented that Lauri got one-half point for trying to clean up her room and that the next time she could get even more by putting the dirty clothes away, hanging her clothes up, and taking a little more time in making the bed.

Both children were in the habit of simply wandering off through the neighborhood without letting the parents know where they were going. On the first day of the contract, a very short practice session was held, in which each child practiced telling their mother and father that they were going somewhere. Both of the parents also practiced reinforcing them for doing this.

When the contract was first explained, neither Eric nor Lauri really understood all of the complexities involved. Lauri, of course, could not follow all the business with numbers and points. She did, however, understand that in the future, teasing, bugging, yelling, hitting, and so forth would lead to Time Out for herself and for Eric, because in the past week she had seen this consequence applied. She also had a vague notion that if she worked hard, she could get more points than Eric and maybe get an afternoon treat and stay up later. Within two or three days, both children understood the details of the contract very well. Each time one of the listed behaviors occurred, it was labeled by the parents, who then immediately walked over and placed an appropriate mark on the contract. The relationship between their behavior and scores then became readily apparent.

Both parents wore wrist counters for the first week in order to keep track of the social reinforcers that they were using. Each of them attempted to provide fifteen reinforcers for each child each day. This, of course, was not always possible, because occasionally the father would come home late and there would be little opportunity to reinforce Lauri, who was in bed by 7:30.

Each day when Eric returned from school at 2:30, the mother would total the point scores for both children and decide whether or not they had earned their special treat. The special treat for the first few weeks consisted of an assortment of candy bars. This back-up reinforcer proved to be something highly prized by both children. Adding up the points at this time often led to a flurry of "good behaviors" as the children wanted to build up points in order to earn the right to leave the yard and play in the neighborhood. In Eric's case, it was necessary to keep his bike chained in the garage during the first week. The first time he was told that he had not earned enough points for his bike, he slipped out of the house, took his bicycle, and was gone for two hours. This was not covered in the contract, but he lost his TV privileges for that evening. The next day his father bought a chain and padlock for the bike. The idea of earning anything was totally new to Eric.

Most aggressive children do not do chores. To Eric and Lauri's parents, it seemed easier to do the chores themselves than to supervise the children while they did what was, at best, an inadequate job. However, eventually it was decided that Lauri should pick up in the living room each day—putting magazines away, emptying ashtrays, and so forth. Eric was to clear the dishes from the table in the evening and stack them on the counter by the sink. During the first week, neither of them earned a full point for their chores.

After the first week or two, both children became thoroughly familiar with the point concept, and it was then possible to make arrangements for long-term contracts. It was agreed, for example, that when both children had earned forty points, they would be accompanied by one of the parents to a Saturday matinee movie. Later still, they earned points for a one-day trip to the coast.

Over a period of weeks the contracts were changed many times. New behaviors were added and old ones removed. The general progress of Eric's programs are noted in the chart below.

As the data show, Eric had his ups and downs—periodically he would have stormy periods when he seemed very much like his old self again. His general pattern of improvement, with the sharp peaks and valleys, is fairly characteristic. A graph for Lauri would look similar to this.

DATA GRAPH

Name _____ Eric _____

Behavior: _____ Compliance and noncompliance _____
_____ contract points _____

Total Points Earned vs Days

As could be expected, after a period of several weeks Eric generally became more predictable and consistent in what he did. The point is quickly reached where the child almost always can be expected to be reasonable and to behave himself. Interestingly enough, as these improvements occurred, Eric also became more affectionate. He was able to touch people without mauling them, to sit with his mother without acting silly, and occasionally to volunteer doing something nice for another family member. It was possible to leave the children with a baby sitter. Even more unusual was the fact that the same baby sitter was willing to return for further engagements.

By the fourth and fifth weeks of the program several neighbors had spontaneously commented to the mother that Eric seemed to be behaving differently now. This is not to say that at this point Eric was a likeable child; he still would be characterized, at best, as "immature." As the aggressive behaviors came under control, the parents shifted the focus of the program to concentrate on reinforcing him for more mature behaviors. Also, the general tone of family interaction had undergone subtle changes by this point. The father commented that he no longer needed some special preparation in order to walk into his own home after work in the evening. The noise level had fallen appreciably, and the crisis rate diminished dramatically. The parents and children had, for the first time, begun to make plans about activities that the family could engage in together on weekends.

Contracting in the Classroom

When it was apparent that the programs being carried out by the parents were partially effective, the school was contacted to determine the possibility of working with Eric in the classroom. The principal and teacher were willing to permit both the collection of observation data in the classroom and the application of the intervention procedures which had been designed particularly for that purpose (Patterson, Cobb, and

143

Ray, 1971; Ray, Shaw, and Cobb, 1970).

Baseline observations in the classroom showed that Eric was spending only thirty percent of his time working on school material, in contrast to the other children, who spent approximately seventy percent of their time "on task." He spent an inordinate amount of time roaming about the classroom teasing and disrupting other children. When asked by the teacher to sit down or to carry out an assignment, he would typically noncomply and become obviously angry as she pushed the point. He was also observed destroying paper and pencils and cutting deep marks into his desk top.

One of the first negotiations involved a contingency for Eric's attacking another child or displaying a severe temper tantrum in the classroom. He was to be taken to the principal's office where he was required to call his parents. His mother would come to school and take him home, where he would be required to scrub the bathroom, and then promptly return him to school.

A small card was taped to Eric's desk each morning. On the first few days of its use, the teacher walked by Eric's desk every five or ten minutes and assigned him points on the basis of the behavior she observed during that time. For example, if he had been sitting at his desk, he could earn three points.

Name Eric							
Behavior (points possible)	M	T	W	T	F	S	S
Sitting at desk (3)							
Working (3)							
Neatness and accuracy (3)							
No teasing or hitting (3)							
Total							

If he had been working during that time, he might earn another three points. He could also earn points for being neat and accurate, and for not disrupting other children. On the first day, the teacher announced to the class that if Eric could earn a full thirty points that morning, they would get out five minutes early for recess. To the delight of all the other children in the group, Eric met that contract and with great pride brought his desk card home that night.

An item was also added to the parents' contract so that he received additional points at home for points earned at school. In this manner the school and the family were working together to provide a supportive program for Eric.

During the first three weeks of the school program, it was necessary for the mother to "run and fetch" Eric only once. On that particular day, the teacher mentioned that he had seemed to come to school with a chip on his shoulder. He scowled fiercely when asked to do perfectly ordinary things and quickly lost a number of points for pushing and teasing other children. Later that morning, he tipped his desk over and threw his books about the room. He was quickly removed from the room and taken to the principal's office. After ten minutes of sitting, he made the telephone call to his mother, which resulted in a thirty-minute session of scrubbing the bathroom.

As the classroom program took effect, Eric spent more time working at his seat, and his work increased dramatically in accuracy and neatness. Arrangements were also made for one of the other children to work with him as he went through programmed materials in arithmetic and reading. Because he was essentially two years behind in his academic work at this point, it was deemed necessary to set up a special summer program for him. In this six-week program, Eric concentrated on reading and arithmetic skills along with a group of children who were having similar problems. The parents were also given special training in using comparable materials. Very short daily practice sessions were held in the home after the parents had received supervision by Karl Skindrud (1971). The program placed a heavy emphasis upon both social reinforcers and points earned for accurate behavior. Six months after the beginning of this classroom intervention program, Eric had accelerated a year and a half in his reading skills and was an accepted member of his peer group in school. When asked about Eric the following year, his new teacher said that he was no particular problem, but she had other boys in the class who were in need of assistance.

Certainly Eric behaves differently now, in both the home and the school. This is not to say that he never hits or pushes or teases; he still does all of these things. What has changed is the rate at which he does them and the settings in which he does them. If another child attacks him, Eric will fight back. Certainly, he still teases his sister Lauri once in a while. He is not a perfect child, but now he is pleasant to be around. He is a human being with whom it is now possible to live and whom, his parents say, it is now possible to love.

Key Ideas in Chapter 12

High rate hitting, teasing, and noncompliance, especially in inappropriate situations, characterize the aggressive child.

Pinpoint one specific, relatively trivial behavior (e.g., noncompliance) to be changed.

Contract for reducing noncompliance:
> identify specific noncompliance behaviors;
> establish a baseline;
> reinforce pro-social behaviors;
> use TO for noncompliance behaviors; and
> chart progress in the program.

The aggressive child's brothers and sisters should be included in the program.

The classroom teacher can use a program similar to that of the parents'.

References

Bandura, A., and Walters, R. H. *Social learning and personality development.* New York: Holt, Rinehart & Winston, 1963.

Ebner, M. Personal communication, 1970.

Homans, G. C. *Social behavior: Its elementary forms.* New York: Harcourt, Brace & World, 1961.

Homme, L., with Csanyi, A. P., Gonzales, M. A., and Rechs, J. R. *How to use contingency contracting in the classroom.* Champaign, Ill.: Research Press, 1970.

Lederer, W. J., and Jackson, D. D. *The mirages of marriage.* New York: Norton, 1968.

Lindsley, O. R. Personal communication, 1970.

Moore, S. Correlates of peer acceptance in nursery school children. *Young Children,* 1967, *22,* 281-297.

Morris, H. H. Aggressive behavior disorders in children: A follow-up study. *American Journal of Psychiatry,* 1956, *112,* 991-997.

Oregon Research Institute (Producer). *A social learning approach to family therapy.* Champaign, Ill.: Research Press, 1974. (Film)

Patterson, G. R. Behavioral techniques based upon social learning: An additional base for developing behavior modification technology. In C. M. Franks (Ed.), *Behavior therapy: Appraisal and status.* New York: McGraw-Hill, 1969. Pp. 341-374.

Patterson, G. R., *Professional guide for* Living with Children *and* Families. Champaign, Ill.: Research Press, 1975.

147

Patterson, G. R., and Cobb, J. A. A dyadic analysis of "aggressive" behaviors: An additional step toward a theory of aggression. In J. P. Hill (Ed.), *Minnesota symposia on child psychology* (Vol. 5). Minneapolis: University of Minnesota Press, 1971. (a)

Patterson, G. R., and Cobb, J. A. The structure of aggressive behavior. In J. F. Knutson (Ed.), *Iowa symposium on the control of aggression.* Iowa City: University of Iowa Press, 1971. (b)

Patterson, G. R., Cobb, J. A., and Ray, R. S. Direct intervention in the classroom. In F. Clark, D. Evans, and L. Hamerlynck (Eds.), *Behavior technology for education.* Calgary, Alberta, Canada: University of Calgary Press, 1971.

Patterson, G. R., Cobb, J. A., and Ray, R. S. A social engineering technology for retraining the families of aggressive boys. In H. E. Adams and I. P. Unikel (Eds.), *Issues and trends in behavior therapy.* Springfield, Ill.: C. C. Thomas, 1973. Pp. 139-224.

Patterson, G. R., Conger, R. E., Reid, J. B., and Jones, R. R. A manual for the professional who trains parents to manage aggressive children. *Oregon Research Institute Research Bulletin,* 1975, *14,* No. 16.

Patterson, G. R., and Gullion, M. E. *Living with children: New methods for parents and teachers* (Rev. ed.). Champaign, Ill.: Research Press, 1971.

Patterson, G. R., and Hops, H. Coercion, a game for two: Intervention techniques for marital conflict. In R. E. Ulrich and P. Mountjoy (Eds.), *The experimental analysis of social behavior.* New York: Appleton-Century-Crofts, 1972.

Patterson, G. R., Littman, R. A., and Bricker, W. Assertive behavior in children: A step toward a theory of aggression. *Monographs of the Society for Research in Child Development,* 1967, *32,* No. 5, (Serial No. 113).

Patterson, G. R., McNeal, S., Hawkins, N., and Phelps, R. Reprogramming the social environment. *Journal of Child Psychology and Psychiatry,* 1967, *8,* 181-195. [Also in: R. Ulrich, T. Stachnick, and J. Mabry (Eds.), *Control of human behavior* (Vol. II). Glenview, Ill.: Scott, Foresman, 1970. Pp. 237-248.]

Patterson, G. R., Ray, R. S., and Shaw, D. A. Direct intervention in families of deviant children. *Oregon Research Institute Research Bulletin,* 1968, *8,* No. 9.

Patterson, G. R., and Reid, J. B. Reciprocity and coercion: Two facets of social systems. In C. Neuringer and J. Michael (Eds.), *Behavior modification in clinical psychology.* New York: Appleton-Century-Crofts, 1970. Pp. 133-177.

Patterson, G. R., Shaw, D. A., and Ebner, M. J. Teachers, peers, and parents as agents of change in the classroom. In F.A.M. Benson (Ed.), *Modifying deviant social behaviors in various classroom settings.* Eugene, Ore.: University of Oregon Department of Special Education, 1969.

Patterson, G. R., and White, G. D. It's a small world: The application of "Time-Out from positive reinforcement." *Oregon Psychological Association Newsletter* (Supplement), 1969, *15*, 2.

Phillips, E. L., and Wolf, M. Modification of behavioral deficiencies in adolescents. Paper presented at the American Psychological Association, San Francisco, 1968.

Ray, R. S., Shaw, D. A., and Cobb, J. A. The Work Box: An innovation in teaching attentional behavior. *The School Counselor,* 1970, *18*, 15-35.

Robins, L. N. *Deviant children grown up: A sociological and psychiatric study of sociopathic personality.* Baltimore: Williams & Wilkins, 1966.

Skindrud, K. Training mothers of disruptive nonreaders in remedial skills: A preliminary study of a home tutoring program. Unpublished manuscript, Oregon Research Institute, Eugene, 1971.

Skinner, B. F. *Science and human behavior.* New York: Appleton-Century-Crofts, 1953.

Stuart, R. B. Operant interpersonal treatment for marital discord. *Journal of Consulting and Clinical Psychology,* 1969, *33*, 675-682.

Ullmann, L. P., and Krasner, L. *A psychological approach to abnormal behavior.* Englewood Cliffs, N. J.: Prentice Hall, 1969.

Wahler, R. G. Behavior therapy with oppositional children: Attempts to increase their parents' reinforcement value. Paper presented at the meeting of the Southeastern Psychological Association, Atlanta, April 1967.

Walker, H. M., Mattson, R. H., and Buckley, N. K. Special class placement as a treatment alternative for deviant behavior in children. In F.A.M. Benson (Ed.), *Modifying deviant social behaviors in various classroom settings.* Eugene, Ore.: University of Oregon Department of Special Education, 1969.

Program Forms

The following program forms are included for your use in implementing a behavior change program. Included are data charts, data graphs, contracts for one behavior, contracts for more than one behavior, and gold star charts.

DATA CARD

Name _____

Behavior: _____

_____

Day	Number of Behaviors	Time Interval	Rate

DATA CARD

Name _____

Behavior: _____

_____

Day	Number of Behaviors	Time Interval	Rate

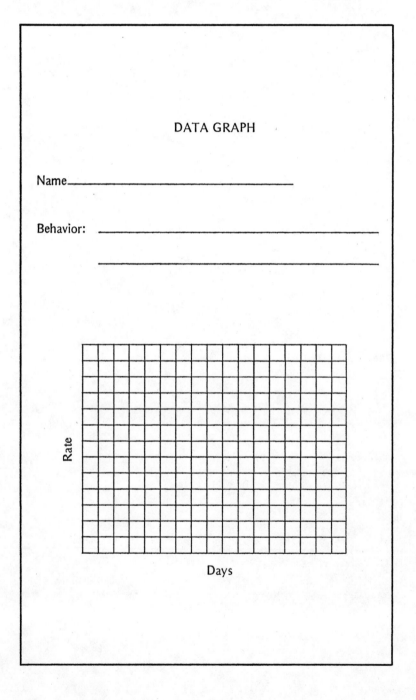

DATA GRAPH

Name_____

Behavior: _____

_____

Rate

Days

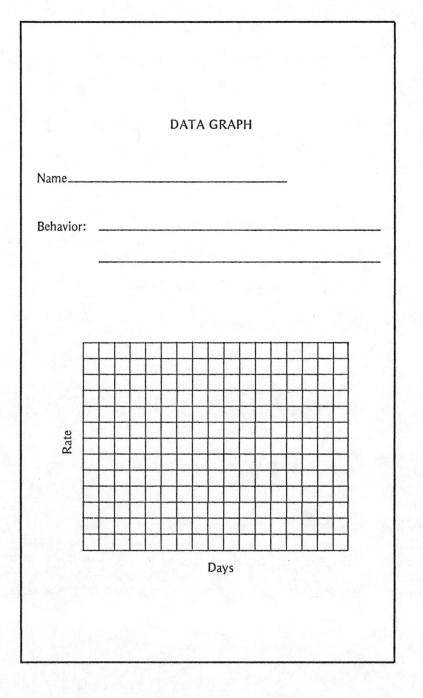

DATA GRAPH

Name_____

Behavior: _____

_____

Rate

Days

Name_____

Behavior: _____

_____

	M	T	W	T	F	S	S
1st week							
2nd week							
3rd week							
4th week							

Consequences:_____

_____

_____

_____

_____

Signed _____

_____

_____

Contract for one behavior

Name_____

Behavior: _____

_____

	M	T	W	T	F	S	S
1st week							
2nd week							
3rd week							
4th week							

Consequences:_____

_____

_____

_____

_____

Signed _____

_____

_____

Contract for one behavior

Name _____

Behavior (points possible)	M	T	W	T	F	S	S

Consequences: _____
_____
_____
_____
_____

Signed _____
_____
_____

Contract for more than one behavior

Name _____

Behavior (points possible)	M	T	W	T	F	S	S

Consequences: _____

Signed _____

Contract for more than one behavior

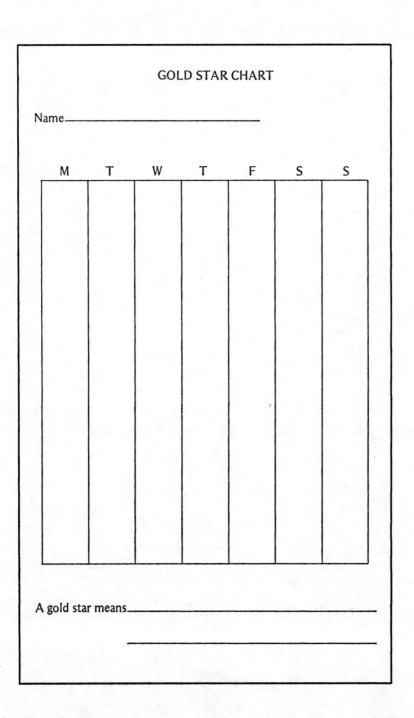

GOLD STAR CHART

Name_____

M	T	W	T	F	S	S

A gold star means_____

_____

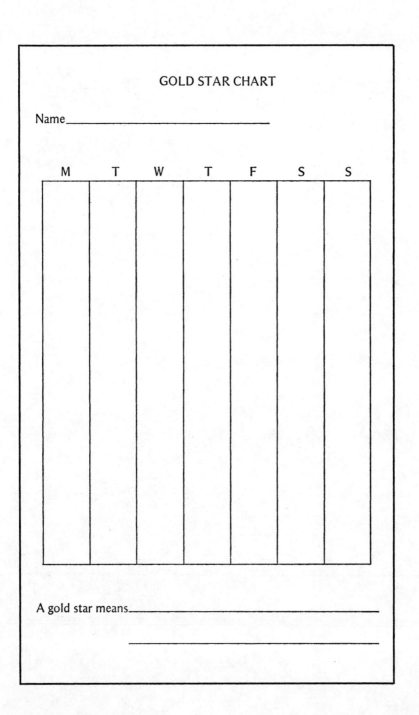

GOLD STAR CHART

Name_____

M	T	W	T	F	S	S

A gold star means_____

_____